WHAT OTHERS ARE SAYING ABOUT THIS BOOK:

"Okerlund promotes a concrete, visible understanding of a fundamental aspect of being human. She makes it deeply empowering and, dare I say, fun to be an introvert."

—**ELIZABETH ERICKSON**, Professor, Minneapolis
College of Art and Design

"Through heart-warming personal stories and solid scientific facts, Nancy Okerlund presents a way for introverts to live with more ease and respect for their naturally complex brains and deeper focus."

—**MARY CARROLL MOORE**, author of *Your Book Starts Here*
and *How to Master Change in Your Life:*
Sixty-seven Ways to Handle Life's Toughest Moments

"I've worked with a Fortune 10 corporation that employs over 100,000 people. Let's assume 25,000 of them are introverts. This is a very extroverted organization and my experience tells me it neither understands nor appreciates its introverted employees. I've often turned "problem managers" into stars just by helping that employee and their boss understand and appreciate what it is to be an introvert. Okerlund's book could have a multi-million dollar beneficial impact on that company's bottom line."

—**JIM EARLEY**, Master Coach, Founder,
Trailblazer Coaching

INTROVERTS *at* EASE

An Insider's Guide to
a Great Life on Your Terms

much love, Gail & Steve!
Nancy

NANCY OKERLUND

DISCLAIMER
This book is designed to provide information on the introverted temperament. It is sold with the understanding that the publisher and author are not engaged in rendering legal or other professional services. If expert assistance is required, the services of a competent professional should be sought. It is not the purpose of this book to provide all the information on this topic that is otherwise available but instead to complement, amplify, and supplement other texts. Every effort has been made to make this book as accurate as possible. However, there may be mistakes, both typographical and in content. Therefore, this book should be used only as a general guide and not as the ultimate source of information on this topic. The purpose of this book is to educate and entertain. The author and publisher shall have neither liability nor responsibility to any person or entity with respect to any loss or damage caused, or alleged to have been caused, directly or indirectly, by the information contained in this book.

Published and printed in the United States of America

ISBN: 146626277X
ISBN-13: 978-1466262775
LCCN: 2011915325

CreateSpace, North Charleston, South Carolina

For my dad and mom,
two exquisitely beautiful introverts

ACKNOWLEDGMENTS

I think it takes a village to create a book. This is a partial list of the village surrounding this one. I give only names because if I spoke to the contributions I've received, this section might get longer than the body of this little book. Some of these contributions were of a moment, others hours or years, some lifelong, all precious:

Allan Cohen, Ann Lovrien, Ann Silver, Bev Lutz, Bob Murray, Brian McKinley, Catharine Reid, Cathy Jacobson, Chuck Levin, Clea McNeely, Davis Taylor, Deb Flaim, Dennis Kearney, Elizabeth Erickson, Emma Palmer, Gail Irish, Graham Van Dixhorn, Greg Beyer, Jan Jarvis, Janet Gannon, Jerry Dorris, Jim Earley, Jody Grack, Jody Thone, John Eggen, Judy Young, Karalee LaBreche, Kathy McKinley, Kate Zehren, Kim Laudert, LA Reding, Laurie Phillips, Lois Egan, Lori Foley, Lorna McLeod, ML Rice, the late Mark Lindblad, Marty Mumma, Mary Carbonneau, Mary Cayan, Mary Carroll Moore, Mary Ellen Lynch, Monica Ochtrup, Mike Baird, Nancy Anderson, Pat Gannon, Pat Kaluza, Randy Okan, Robert Middleton, Robin Boe, Ruth Hayden, Steve Budas, Susan Hubbard, Suzanne Fry, and Zoe Nicholie;

My wonderful and amazing coaching clients, past and present, introverts and extroverts alike;

The faithful and inspiring readers of my electronic newsletter, *The Introvert Energizer;*

And, of course, my beloved family.

Anyone who feels his or her name is missing, please know you're in my heart.

CONTENTS

Introduction . . . .*ix*

Slow Is Beautiful! 1
Collecting Hap Hits 4
Learning the Easy Way 8
Extroverting at the Fair 11
The Introvert Way 15
Going Slower 19
Smiling Patience 22
Amused Curiosity and Lame Jokes 25
Twelve Things and a Long Hot Bath 30
Introvertly Happy 33
Doing the Right Thing 37
No! No! A Thousand Times, No!! 41
Enough 44
The Introvert Smile 47
Stewarding Our Energy 51
Going on Vacation 54
"Feel the Fear and Do It Anyway" 57
Where's the Downtime?! 61
Working Happily Ever After 65
Introvert Grandmother 68
The Care and Feeding of Introverts 71
Write On! 75
Introvert Small Talk 78
Drained by Joy 81
"Slow Down and Feel the Energy" 86

CONTENTS (CONTINUED)

Quiet Leadership .89

"This Is the Time for Introverts!" 93

Bathtub Reading .96

Introvert Response Ability 100

Spotting Introverts 103

"Ask Without Hesitation..." 107

Deep Buddy 110

Nowhere to Go, Nothing to Do 113

Diving Deep and Surfacing 116

Six Years of Introvert Bliss 119

Around the World in Eighty Hours 123

"She's Very Ingoing!" 128

Introvert/Extrovert Fusion 131

Walking Slow 135

That Inner (Introvert) Child 138

Introvert on the Road 142

"What Shall I Do with All My Books?" 145

The Introvert with the Kitchen Timer 149

Introvert Parents off the Hook 153

Inside My Head, Reflecting 156

Introvert on Staycation 159

People Lovers 163

On Twitter 166

Friendship by Phone 169

Final Thoughts 172

About the Author *173*

INTRODUCTION

$\mathscr{I}$ fell in love with myself as an introvert almost overnight. In the spring of 2003, I found out that introverts are "hardwired"—it's physical. It was almost as simple as that. I quickly realized I'd been trying to be an extrovert, unconsciously, my whole life. As soon as I grasped the physiology of introversion and how it connects to my life experience literally moment by moment, I relaxed—and fell in love with myself, the introvert. And the feeling hasn't stopped.

It wasn't that I didn't know about my introversion. Like millions of Americans, I'd taken the Myers-Briggs Type Indicator (MBTI) early in my work life, decades before. It pronounced me an introvert, and for a few weeks after the training that went with the inventory, I remember identifying as a "tent thinker." But that faded into the background fast, and before long I was once again oblivious to my "preference" for introversion, as it was described.

INTROVERTS *at* EASE

This small book is a collection of articles from my electronic newsletter (ezine), *The Introvert Energizer*. I began it writing in 2007, some years into being fascinated with my coming into consciousness about my introvert self and with the experiences of my life coaching clients, whose processes often seemed to mirror mine remarkably.

I coined the term "conscious introvert," because I've been so moved by the difference it has made in my life to have this new level of self-awareness about my body and mind (and heart and spirit, to be honest). I went from a vague sense of something's being wrong with me to the sudden realization that the ways in which I felt abnormal or out of place had to do with the way my body *naturally* functions in the extroverted nature of our culture. My introversion had been normalized! (Curious that I didn't really discover my "problem" until I saw the solution.)

The strengths of introverts are many. We tend to be observant, thoughtful, and good listeners. We have a strong ability to focus and to concentrate. We tend to be cooperative and responsible, studious, good planners. We tend to think outside the box and to persevere. We tend to be independent and have the strength to make unpopular decisions. We recognize and accept the complexity and vastness of things. We know how to set a slower pace. And we tend to be very self-aware.

The dilemma we face is that American culture is very extroverted, and we're expected to plug ourselves into that norm as extroverts. No small feat in itself, with our introverted bodies, but this expectation is complicated by the reality that temperament isn't given much recognition as being fundamental to our identity. Everybody knows the words "introvert" and "extrovert," but we don't much view ourselves through that lens. And, of course, long-standing negative assumptions and stereotypes about introverts further complicate the dilemma.

A basic difference between introverts and extroverts is where they focus their attention. Extroverts focus on the external world of people, places, and things: the outer. Introverts focus on the internal world of thoughts, feelings, impressions: the inner. I would offer this book even if it were only a contribution to the pursuit of more ease and enjoyment for introverts. But, in a broader stroke, I believe the world is out of balance—too much outer, not enough inner—for which we pay a big price. In the words of Peter Whybrow, MD, author of *American Mania—When More Is Not Enough*: "Despite an astonishing appetite for life, more and more Americans are feeling overworked and dissatisfied. In the world's most affluent nation, epidemic rates of stress, anxiety, depression, obesity, and time urgency are now grudgingly accepted as part of everyday existence—they signal the American Dream gone awry."

I believe the world is longing for what introverts have: more inner energy. I believe the world is longing for a dynamic balance of inner and outer energy and that such a balance will go a long way toward addressing the critical issues of our time: poverty, economic instability, ill health, war, climate change, and an undercurrent of fear. I'm advocating for a gentle sea change: conscious introverts, conscious extroverts, a culture that is extrovert- and introvert-friendly.

What do we have to gain? Introverts who are thriving: at ease, energized, effective, enjoying life. Everybody happier, introverts and extroverts alike, contributing naturally. Organizations tapping into excellence. The world addressing its challenges skillfully.

But the purpose of this book is not to make the case for such a sea change. It is rather about considering the possibility of becoming more conscious of being an introvert, a "conscious introvert," and what that mind-set has to offer.

The strategy I propose has five aspects:

1. Understanding the physiology of introversion
2. Reframing introversion as an asset
3. Managing energy skillfully
4. Finding introvert ways of doing things
5. Becoming skillful at "extroverting"

This is an individual process and not linear. In sharing my own process, I hope you see yourself as normal on a continuum of physical differences, and I hope you recognize the constant impact of these physical attributes. I hope you become even more aware of your introvert strengths.

I hope you recognize the importance of paying attention to your energy and of getting enough downtime to reenergize. I hope you are encouraged to nurture your own way of doing things rather than consciously or unconsciously trying to be an extrovert. And I hope you see extroverting as a set of skills to be used when they're called for rather than as the only way to behave in an extroverted society.

I have admiration and gratitude for the work of Marti Olsen Laney, the psychologist who has synthesized the brain and temperament research on introversion and extroversion and offers a comprehensive profile of the introvert experience in her books *The Introvert Advantage—How to Thrive in an Extrovert World* and *The Hidden Gifts of the Introverted Child—Helping Your Child Thrive in an Extroverted World*. In those books, I learned about the longer, more complex, introvert brain pathway. This revelation was the beginning of my new relationship with myself. Laney's books offer fascinating and accessible information on how introvert bodies work. You'll see her referenced often in these pages.

You'll find practical ideas for extroverts as well as introverts. I write my electronic newsletter for introverts and extroverts, because all extroverts have introverts in their lives. It is my conviction that the better we understand each other, the stronger the potential to maximize the gifts of introversion and extroversion. Conscious introverts and conscious extroverts can interact well together.

I want this to be a book introverts can pick up and be encouraged by in a moment, as they can by reading each issue of my ezine. I want this to be a book that can educate introverts and extroverts about the physicality of being either an introvert or an extrovert and about the inaccurate profile of introverts, correcting and replacing it with an accurate one.

I see the clear possibility of a healthy, dynamic balance of inner and outer—for the sake of introverts at ease and for the sake of the world working *beautifully*.

Slow Is Beautiful!

One morning a couple weeks ago, I woke up early, as usual, and remembered I had no commitments for about three hours. It was a weekday, and for no particular reason, I suddenly decided to pretend I was on vacation for the next couple hours. So instead of dragging myself out of bed, I just lay there and wondered what would happen next.

What I mean by "dragging" is that even though I consider myself good at getting up early in the morning, quickly, it's never fun. I always wish it could be spread out over about two hours. And that's what happened. For awhile, I dozed. When I was really awake—I could tell because my eyes were staying open :-)—I daydreamed.

Pretty soon I felt like reading, so I did for maybe ten or fifteen minutes. After that was probably another little stretch of wandering thoughts—I don't quite remember—but at some point I knew I wanted to get up, so I

1

did. I continued meandering into the morning, and by the time my three-hour vacation was over, I was a happy camper.

I remember comparing morning routines with my friend Dennis some years ago. (Dennis is an extrovert.) He said he loves getting up in the morning—he jumps out of bed and immediately feels ready to roll. I remember not quite believing him. I'm not that much older than Dennis, and he has a very busy life. How could he possibly love jumping out of bed?! And what was I doing wrong?

That was before I knew about the physical differences between introverts and extroverts. To make a long story short—about our brain chemistry and nervous systems—research on temperament is showing that even though introverts and extroverts have the same equipment, we use it quite differently. For instance, introverts rely mainly on the neurotransmitter (brain chemical) acetylcholine. Extroverts use dopamine. Acetylcholine works to slow down the body so the brain can concentrate. Dopamine is about action, movement, pleasure. Dopamine says, "If it feels good, do it!" Acetylcholine says, "Let's think about it."

Another difference is that introverts naturally operate more from the part of the autonomic nervous system (the parasympathetic, to get technical) that's about rest and restoration. Extroverts operate more from the other side of the autonomic nervous system (the sympathetic), the one that's in charge of the "fight, flight, or fright" response. It's primed for action.

Human beings are complex, and every person is unique, but what this boils down to is that, in general, introverts have a naturally slower pace than 50 to 75 percent of the population. And we have to be more conscious about moving our bodies than extroverts, because their brains/nervous systems are set up to move, in a sense, automatically. We have to think about it!

The moral of the story for introverts? Slow down—and enjoy it! We live in a fast-moving world that unconsciously expects us all to keep up with its pace. Even extroverts, who are wired to thrive on stimulation, feel overstimulated these days. I have a better context for understanding how I am in the morning than I did when Dennis and I compared notes, but I'm still in the process of giving myself permission to find the ways to go at my natural pace. Slow is beautiful, I say!

End of food for thought, on to some practical ideas:

A Practical Idea *for* Introverts

Think of an activity that often or always feels rushed for you and, on purpose, give yourself the luxury of doing it in an unrushed way. If it feels good, do it that way again sometime.

A Practical Idea *for* Extroverts

Compare notes with an introvert in your life on morning routines—how you feel, what you like to do, what you don't like to do.

Collecting Hap Hits

My dad, Harry Sherman, was a master vegetable gardener. He died four years ago in July at the age of ninety. This year on the anniversary of his passing, I decided to spend the day gardening. I'm not a master gardener of anything, but I love being in the dirt, and I love to weed. So our yard full of flower beds, mainly tended by my gardening-loving partner, was just the place for me.

My dad was an introvert, and as I slowly, carefully weeded, deadheaded, and did a little transplanting (with instruction!), I compared notes on two introverts and their gardening styles—my dad and me.

Introverts are known for their ability to focus and to concentrate deeply for long periods. The ability has to do with the predominant introvert brain chemical, acetylcholine, and with the introvert's brain's experiencing more blood flow and higher activity in the frontal lobes. As brain experts say, the brain is always torn between speed and accuracy, and the introvert's brain prefers accuracy. (Focus and concentration are good for that.)

My dad was an introvert gardener. His concentration was endless. In early winter, he studied piles of seed catalogs and ordered regularly changing varieties of tomatoes, beans, eggplants, and all the rest—and tracked the changes from year to year. In late winter/early spring, he raised hundreds of baby plants from seed, treating each one like a little princess or prince, it seemed to me.

And from the time the garden was planted—and it wasn't small—he could give a detailed report on the well-being of everything in it, whenever you asked. His focus seemed almost single-minded, into at least late September. (My mother had a love-hate relationship with the garden.) He always moved at a slow pace, even when he was young, and seemed to pause often, leaning on the hoe, looking out onto the prairie.

He successfully used the garden as a way to get lots of alone time. Except for short visits from the outside world, it was his private space. I sensed a certain sadness in him at the relative lack of attention he gave the rest of the yard, but his priority was clear—and it wasn't trees, grass, or flowers.

I, on the other hand, am an introvert *non*gardener. I love the idea of gardening, and I love the actual experience, once I'm doing it. But between the idea and the experience is a big lake of ambivalence. Here's what I can say about my ambivalence: that natural introvert tendency to focus and to go deep plus the part of me that loves being in the dirt could easily mean I walk out into the backyard to "do a little weeding" and not surface for three hours.

That could be wonderful, except I haven't made gardening a priority, so my life isn't set up to spend hours and hours doing it. I've been living in the fog of ambivalence. Attracted but not committed, indecisive and not very happy about it.

For my dad, growing things was in his blood. It had to be a priority. He must have recognized that and gave himself over to it. And he got untold pleasure from the experience, even in the face of frequent North Dakota droughts.

Here's why it's important for introverts to be clear about our priorities. Researchers have a term called "hap hits" that refers to a feeling of satisfaction, enjoyment—"hits" of happiness. Introverts get hap hits from experiencing things in depth. Extroverts get hap hits from lots of stimulation. Typically they thrive on a wider net of experiences than introverts. As introverts, if we spread ourselves too thin and don't indulge our natural inclination to focus and to concentrate in depth, we miss out on hap hits and probably also feel overstimulated—a double whammy.

As for me and my day of gardening, I got a lot of hap hits. I let myself go at my own pace rather than having a goal of weeding the whole yard. Each little section I worked on was a pleasure. It was tending in-depth! And I got to be with my thoughts and feelings about my dad, lots of introspection, in the dirt. :-)

And now, a few weeks later, I can see that my lake of ambivalence has shrunk to more of a pond. I'm not a gardener, but I do spend time in the dirt. End of food for thought, on to some practical ideas:

A Practical Idea *for* Introverts

Notice where in your life you focus and concentrate for long periods of time. If it's not happening to your satisfaction, choose something attractive to focus on and carve out some time to concentrate on it with some depth. Go for hap hits! Or, if you're tired out from trying to squeeze your concentration into a too-busy life, take a look at your priorities. Do you have too many?

A Practical Idea *for* Extroverts

Spend ten or fifteen minutes listening to an introvert in your life talk to you about something he or she loves to do.

Learning
the Easy Way

’m on retreat in South Carolina on five hundred acres of virgin forest. As I sit in the morning shade at an old picnic table on the edge of Long Lake, a little alligator swims by. Beyond the lake is the ocean. I’m here for a week, no schedule, and I’m watching myself.

I’ve brought eighteen books and several magazines on my retreat. And since arriving I’ve bought a few books, so the total is up a little. (I love books.) I’m watching myself to see what I can notice about how I balance my need for rest and renewal with my love of learning. Will it happen?!

Introverts tend to love learning. New technology in brain scanning has let researchers watch the flow of blood in the brains of introverts and extroverts. The extrovert pathway flows to the areas where sensory processing happens. Extrovert brains welcome lots of stimulation from the outside world and process it quickly.

8

The introvert path is longer, more complicated, and focused internally. It goes to the parts of the brain involved with such internal experiences as remembering, solving problems, and planning. Introvert brains are busy. They're constantly comparing and contrasting what they're taking in with the introverts' own personal reactions.

Without enough input to fuel their thoughts, introverts can get bored and frustrated. But too much input too fast can be overwhelming and not leave enough time to do all that reflecting. Meanwhile, extroverts are out looking for more experiences.

I do love learning, and one of my favorite ways is through books. The most exciting part of packing for the trip was choosing which books to bring, especially with a whole week of open-ended time ahead of me. But was my big book appetite setting me up for being overstimulated, even on an unscheduled retreat?

Here's what I'm noticing: balance is happening! On the introvert/extrovert continuum, I'd put myself quite a ways from center on the introvert side. For one thing, that means my need for peace-and-quiet recharging time is fairly high.

Early in the week, the books sorted themselves out. A few came as references, and they've been helpful. A few more quickly backed out of the picture. I could tell I didn't want to read them this week. Some became "dippers," and a couple got the job of "light bedtime." Five really grabbed my attention for new learning. Of the whole pile, I have the goal of finishing only one while I'm here, and it's short.

I've had lots of time for looking out on the lake from the screened porch, listening to the ocean in the background. Quiet walks in the forest. Unhurried cooking. Many rounds of my Aunt Annabelle's hardest version of solitaire interspersed with my old friend, the traveling electronic Yahtzee game. Trips to the beach to jump in the ocean. Leisurely conversations with my partner.

And even some extroverting sprinkled in. A few small concerts and films here at the retreat center, some afternoon tea times, and one trip into town for lunch.

All in all, very satisfying. Resting, learning, finding my own pace in a beautiful setting. An introvert's delight, I might say. :-)

End of food for thought, on to some practical ideas:

A PRACTICAL IDEA *for* INTROVERTS

Assume you're out of touch with your natural pace (the world runs on extrovert time) and spend a weekend investigating it.

A PRACTICAL IDEA *for* EXTROVERTS

Compare notes with an introvert in your life on your ideas of a great weekend.

Extroverting
at the Fair

A couple weeks ago, I spent six hours in front of a roasted corn stand at the Minnesota State Fair. I was a recycling volunteer. My job was to encourage the corn eaters to put their cobs in the compost bin rather than the garbage can. This stand sells an average of ten thousand ears of corn every day during the fair, so I'd signed myself up for a day of "extroverting."

For introverts, extroverting requires energy. I think of the word as a way to describe introverts doing things that are more natural to extroverts. It can include lots of different activities—standing for hours in the middle of a stream of people on their way to buy corn on the cob certainly qualifies, especially if you're trying to talk to them!

Energy is a key issue for introverts. We get ours from inside, from the world of our ideas, feelings, impressions. And we need a low-stimulation

11

environment—some form of "peace and quiet"—to get recharged. We live in a world that's heavily influenced by extroverts, who get energized by the outside world: activities, people, places, things. For an extrovert, standing in a crowd talking to people about their corn cobs is a way to get energy. For an introvert, it spends energy.

The world tends to operate extrovert-style, and people don't talk much about being introverts or extroverts. So you may never have even heard, much less considered, the word "extroverting." It's not that introverts don't have the equipment for extroverting—our bodies are just less naturally inclined to do so. Some extroverting is unavoidable in today's world—a long airplane trip, for instance, with its crowds and cramped quarters. Some of us work in environments that require almost continuous extroverting.

Having good extroverting skills is part of what I consider being a conscious introvert. It gives us more choice and freedom of movement in the world. But we can't afford to be energy spenders in the same way extroverts can. Extroverts naturally get energy from interacting with people, places, and things. It's easier for them to stay replenished just by being in the world. Research on introverts and extroverts demonstrates that it takes more time for introverts to restore our energy and it flows out faster than in extroverts. And we can't get replenished in the middle of the state fair!

So introverts do better when we keep track of our energy and practice energy conservation! It's been years since I spent a day at the state fair. Before I knew about introvert energy conservation, I'd go every year and loved being there, even though it was overstimulating. But the next day (or maybe two), I'd feel like I'd been run over by a truck, so I finally stopped going.

This year, I knew I wanted to go as soon as I got the invitation to be a compost volunteer. It was a chance to do something I feel strongly about, a chance to support the work of one of my good friends, and a chance to spend the day with another of my good friends. Very worth it. I could easily have overdone it, though. When I went off duty, even though my energy was gone, I was tempted to take a side trip into the Butterfly House. :-) But I went home instead, to take care of my tired introvert self, very happy that I'd gone and also very happy to be home.

End of food for thought, on to some practical ideas:

SOME PRACTICAL IDEAS *for* INTROVERTS

If your life currently requires a lot of extroverting and you don't get enough downtime, choose one day to deliberately do things differently and find some ways to pamper your introvert self.

Practice introvert energy conservation with an upcoming extroverting event. Plan to have downtime beforehand and afterward—and do it!

A Practical Idea *for* Extroverts

Show off your sophisticated understanding of introverts (I'm not kidding!) by explaining to an introvert in your life that you're aware of the difference between introvert and extrovert energy and ask how that person likes to get downtime.

THE INTROVERT WAY

*I*n August, I spent a whole day at the state fair extroverting, and I had a great time, even though it wiped me out. One evening last week, I spent three hours in extrovert mode, and I didn't have a great time—but I learned a lesson. I went to a networking event, one of those gatherings explicitly designed for exchanging information about yourself with others, for the purpose of advancing your business.

Now, I already know I don't like networking events, but I decided to go because this wasn't just a regular networking meeting. It included a presentation about communication from an organization whose work I'm interested in, so it offered the possibility of some new information or perspective. And in the meantime, I thought maybe I'd discover that I've outgrown my distaste for networking meetings.

I felt quite confident as I arrived, although not exactly comfortable, because it was in a part of town I don't know well, the building was totally unfamiliar, and I suspected I would know no one, which turned out to be true (three situations that don't create comfort for introverts).

But I felt confident, because I had been psyching myself up for this evening. My game plan was to be myself as an introvert and see what happened. I got some appetizers, sat down at a table with an empty spot, and introduced myself. When someone asked me why I was there, I told her I'm an introvert and that I'm always exploring ways to be out in the world.

Lo and behold, it turned out all three of my tablemates had already reported to each other that they're introverts! Off we went into a conversation about being introverts. How cool was that? My game plan was turning out better than I had expected! But as the evening continued, I wasn't happy. I was participating appropriately. I might have even been mistaken for an extrovert. And I had that good start, talking to my introvert tablemates.

At the state fair, I was in a situation I'd call extreme extroverting—initiating short conversations with a continuous stream of people for hours. It was exhausting, but it was also satisfying. At the networking event, I was in a fairly low-key setting, yet I was feeling less satisfied by the minute.

"Conscious introvert" is a term I've coined to describe an intentional way of being an introvert. It has five aspects: understanding the physiology of introverts, framing being an introvert as an asset, making reenergizing a high priority, creating introvert ways of doing things, and developing extroverting skills.

By the time I left—without lingering for one moment—the lesson was beginning to dawn on me. It had to do with creating introvert ways of doing things. I saw more clearly than ever that networking events are extroverted in nature. The presentation part of this evening included some good coaching on the difference between authentic and inauthentic networking, but the context was still extroversion: a group of people having brief, to-the-point interactions, as efficiently as possible. Generally speaking, an introvert would prefer to have an in-depth conversation with one person.

But the lesson for me was this: behaving like an introvert is good for my soul. Extroverting at the fair was good for my soul, too. But the more I do things my own introvert way, the better I feel. Life is complex, each person is unique, and there isn't any one "introvert way." But for me, when it comes to networking meetings, the costs outweigh the benefits. Behaving like an introvert means staying away from them. (Unless I change my mind.)

To create our own introvert ways of doing things in an extroverted culture is not a small assignment. I think it requires that we trust ourselves and risk feeling even more out-of-the-ordinary. But what have we got to lose? Unhappiness. :-)

End of food for thought, on to some practical ideas:

A PRACTICAL IDEA *for* INTROVERTS

Pick an activity in your life that feels unsatisfying and look to see how it connects with being an introvert. If there's no connection (dissatisfaction happens for many reasons), pick a different activity. When you have one, see if you can find a more introvert-friendly, comfortable way of doing it.

A PRACTICAL IDEA *for* EXTROVERTS

Pick one of your favorite things to do and think about how an introvert would relate to it. If it seems like an extrovert activity, how could it be adapted to be more satisfying for an introvert?

GOING SLOWER

*T*oday I'm watching myself rush. What's interesting is that I'm doing it without time pressure. I have only one appointment—the rest of the day is unscheduled—yet my body is still hurrying. When I notice I'm hurrying, I slow down. I let myself walk slower. (This happens every few minutes.) I catch myself speeding as I wash my lunch dishes and ease up. I'm on my way to the freeway when I remember I'd rather take the scenic route to the library—city streets, slower, more relaxing—so I do.

I love going slower. (I notice I don't want to say, "I love going slow.") What I don't like is hurrying. And I don't like the assumption that I *should* be hurrying, which, unfortunately, seems to be built into my operating system.

Whenever I realize I'm hurrying and allow myself go slower, always, I notice it first in my body. I think I experience what the brain researchers

19

call a "hap hit," a noticeable feeling of satisfaction, a "hit" of happiness, even if it sometimes lasts only a fleeting moment. I'm guessing one thing introverts and extroverts have in common is that none of us likes to hurry as a way of life.

Out of curiosity, I looked up "hurry" in the dictionary, thinking it would say something like going faster than normal or faster than you want to. But it wasn't until the third definition or so that going too fast came up, so maybe I'm wrong about extroverts, because the basic definition was simply about going quickly.

And pace, according to temperament research, is different for introverts and extroverts. Generally speaking, extroverts do have a faster pace than introverts because of differences in brain chemistry and in how we use the autonomic nervous system. Introverts and extroverts are in the same boat, though, when it comes to my definition of "hurrying as a lifestyle": going faster than you want to more often than you like. Nobody likes that. It's built into the definition! And my hunch is that it's not just introverts who face the challenge of hurrying as a lifestyle.

But help is on the way! Some time ago, I read a book called *In Praise of Slowness*, by Carl Honoré. It was published in 2004 and describes the international "Slow Movement," which is taking many forms around the world. For instance: the seven-hundred-plus member Sloth Club in Japan, the Society for the Deceleration of Time in Europe, Citta Slow ("Slow Cities") in Italy, slow-food activists all over the world, and millions of people slowly doing their yoga right here in the United States.

I'm curious about the makeup of this multifaceted movement. Is it mainly introverts, quietly taking things into our own hands? Extroverts deciding the speed of life has gotten out of control and mobilizing? Introverts and extroverts organically collaborating? I like to say that I believe the world is longing for more "introvert energy"—more reflection, more quiet, a slower pace. I'm hoping the Slow Movement is an introvert-extrovert collaboration, because I know introverts have natural talent to contribute to it.

Meanwhile, back in my own body (which played three games of solitaire really fast today), I've got two things going for me. One is that I love those hap hits I get when I slow down. The other is that I've declared my intention to let my life be slower. An intention can be very powerful.

End of food for thought, on to a practical idea:

A PRACTICAL IDEA *for* INTROVERTS *and* EXTROVERTS

Think about the amount of hurrying in your life. If it's about
right, take a moment to feel satisfied. If it's more than you like,
set an intention to slow your pace down a notch or two.
Find a way to remind yourself about your intention once
a week—and see what happens!

SMILING PATIENCE

*T*his week, I'm practicing "smiling patience"—patience, with a smile. It's been five days since I finished a six-day qigong retreat. I'm smiling for two reasons: I'm happy, and during the retreat I learned that the face includes lots of energy meridians, and smiling is good for them, good for building my energy. I'm practicing patience, because it's challenging to be back in regular life after six days of almost nonstop stimulation. My introvert self would like to be on another retreat right now, absorbing all that input.

"Qigong" (pronounced "chee-gung") is Chinese and translates loosely as energy work. It's an ancient study, considered the great-grandfather of all Eastern healing and martial arts techniques.

These days I seem to be living my life as an introvert laboratory, so I arrived at the retreat with curiosity but also some uncertainty. In August, I'd spent a week on retreat in a forest with essentially one other person.

22

It was quiet and peaceful and wonderful. Now I'd signed myself up to be on retreat with about 180 people in a conference center. Could it be a good experience for an introvert? Would it be wonderful? The answer is yes—it was good, and it was wonderful.

My biggest concern was that I'd be overstimulated—too many people, too much information, not enough alone time to maintain a good level of energy. Energy is such an important subject for introverts, given our physical makeup and our need for low-stimulation environments to recharge our energy. I realize, somewhat in hindsight, that it was maybe even a *brilliant* decision for me, as an introvert, to go on an "energy-work" retreat! What I learned about working with my energy far exceeded my expectations. And we were actively practicing qigong, so even in the company of 180 people, I was surprisingly able to maintain good energy—with some ups and downs. :-)

I also took good care of myself: I had my own room, I brought my own pillows (introverts like familiarity), and I gave myself permission to be as quiet as I wanted to. No trying to act like an extrovert this week for me! All in all, it was an extraordinary experience. (The Spring Forest Qigong Retreat was a collaboration between Spring Forest Qigong and Learning Strategies Corporation, two organizations I highly recommend for introverts and extroverts.)

But now that I'm home, about that patience. It was a very stimulating week! The days started at 7:00 a.m. and ended after 10:00 p.m. I took seventy-eight pages of notes (I counted them just for fun). I used my body in many new ways. I laughed a lot. I mingled with 180 fascinating people who came from all over the United States and around the world. By the time I got home, I was ready for some serious downtime, but it wasn't to be had.

So I'm practicing patience. On Monday, instead of starting this article, I went shopping for long underwear, slowly. (Winter is coming to Minnesota.) On Tuesday, instead of starting this article, I went for a long walk in a marsh, slowly. Today, I'm writing, but I've decided this newsletter can come out a little late. And I'm smiling.

End of food for thought, on to a practical idea:

A PRACTICAL IDEA *for* INTROVERTS *and* EXTROVERTS

Visit the Web sites of Spring Forest Qigong (www.springforestqigong.com) and Learning Strategies Corporation (www.learningstrategies.com). Master Chunyi Lin, founder of Spring Forest Qigong, became a certified international qigong master after many years of study in China. He teaches four levels of qigong and has created a series of home learning materials that are available through Learning Strategies. He lives in Minnesota.

Besides publishing the Spring Forest Qigong programs, Learning Strategies Corporation, also located in Minnesota, is internationally known for its innovative self-growth programs—for instance, photoreading, which teaches you to read twenty-five thousand words per minute. (Yes, twenty-five thousand!) I learned to photoread many years ago and highly recommend it.

Amused Curiosity
and Lame Jokes

I notice my relationship to energy is changing, for the better. I wonder if I have more of it or if I'm using what I have differently. Last week, I received a message from someone who asked, "Where can one find physical energy when one absolutely has to have some, in order to cope with the demands of contemporary life, from which there is ultimately no escape? . . . I had hoped you had discovered some new source of energy for introverts to tap into—other than the necessary downtime."

Still fresh from my six-day qigong retreat, in a way I felt like I *had* discovered a new source of energy (even though I started learning qigong in the early 1990s). Six days of immersion in that world of "energy work" was no small thing.

Marti Olsen Laney, in *The Introvert Advantage*, calls extroverts "energy spenders" and introverts "energy conservers." Extroverts get energy easily from people, places, and things. Interacting with the world is like being plugged into a continuous source of energy. Extroverts can afford to be spenders. We energy conservers (introverts) play quite a different ball game. We get our energy from the inside, from our thoughts, feelings, and impressions. We're not plugged into that ongoing "worldly" energy source. In fact, lots of stimulation drains us. And our nervous systems need peace and quiet to complete the internal energizing.

Does that mean introverts get to pick from two hard options: being overstimulated or being cloistered away to have downtime? I certainly hope not, and I don't think so. It's been several years since I started consciously relating to myself as an introvert. I think that recognition was a big first step. One of our challenges is that introvert vs. extrovert isn't really on the world's radar screen yet.

I felt a big relief at understanding the new research about the physiology of introverts and extroverts. And I started to regularly think about myself as an introvert. As an introvert, maybe I was invisible to the world, but not to myself! I began turning into a conscious introvert. (And it started happening with my coaching clients.) Even though I hadn't particularly identified with the negative stereotypes about introverts, I didn't have many positive traits in my mind, either. And I felt out of sync with the world on a regular basis.

That feeling changed. As I got a sense of the introvert profile, it wasn't long before I felt downright proud of my new identity. And even if the world still seemed to be marching to a different beat, I didn't seem as out of step. I stopped feeling wrong (and confused) and started feeling different (and curious).

I'd always managed to carve out downtime, no doubt a survival tactic, which chronically cut into my sleep time at both ends. With my new introvert identity, I gradually stopped thinking that needing downtime is a weakness. I don't know that I get any more these days than I used to, but I make no apologies (and I do get more sleep!). I started to be very curious about how to behave as an introvert when not in downtime. With my developing understanding of the United States as a big extrovert of a country, I felt more relief and more permission to feel different instead of wrong.

But how to act "different"?! Initially I think it was mainly an internal process, watching myself to see what I could notice about how I behave as an introvert—being kinder and more compassionate with myself when I noticed my awkwardness at small talk or my discomfort in new surroundings, for instance. And just wondering, if I stopped unconsciously trying to fit in by being an extrovert, then how could I behave as an introvert?!

That's an ongoing question, but a pleasant one. Instead of the anxious confusion I lived in as an unconscious introvert, now I notice a lot of amused curiosity. I make lame jokes with myself—and sometimes others :-)—about how an introvert would do this or that. I find myself feeling good-natured and open-hearted in overstimulating situations, like crowds, for instance. A few years ago, I leaned more toward criticism and whining.

Gradually I'm feeling more and more ease at just being myself, including going at that slower introvert pace. (Last week I told you I brought my own pillows to the qigong retreat. The fuller truth is that I also brought a down comforter and a small carload of other stuff to help me feel comfortable away from home.)

Then there's extroverting, another important part of being a conscious introvert. More amused curiosity and more lame jokes here. One thing I notice is that finding my introvert way to do things is a companion of developing extroverting skills. In any given moment, it seems, I have the choice to act the introvert or the extrovert way, often an interesting decision.

For me, I think the biggest shift in this area is that I now make a clear distinction between having extroverting skills and living an extrovert lifestyle. And I'm no longer trying to live like an extrovert. (At the moment, the cutting edge for me with extroverting is to be fluent at "speaking extrovert"—easy with small talk, shorter sentences, louder voice, switching subjects quickly.) So I'm what I call a conscious introvert. I've reframed introversion. Not only am I very aware of it, but I love being an introvert and consider it a wonderful asset. I manage my energy respectfully. I'm finding my own introvert ways of being in the world, and I'm working on my extroverting skills.

My relationship to energy has changed. I don't know whether I have more or that I'm using what I have differently. Whichever it is, I'm having a good time. As for discovering some new source of energy for introverts to tap into, as a matter of fact, the qigong retreat has stimulated my thinking along those lines. I think the sky's probably the limit!

End of food for thought, on to some practical ideas:

A Practical Idea *for* Introverts

Think of five things you enjoy about being an introvert. Keep
them in mind for sharing in a conversation when the time is right.
(A contribution to the cause of more visibility for introverts!)

A Practical Idea *for* Extroverts

Wonder about what it would mean to be a conscious extrovert.

Twelve Things and a Long Hot Bath

*T*his morning, I took a long hot bath. It was a last-minute decision that overrode my to-do list and involved some quick rethinking about my day's schedule. Shortly before Thanksgiving, my daily to-do lists start getting bigger and more challenging, and they stay that way until the end of the year. Yesterday was a full, productive weekend day, and it was satisfying: a good combination of working, playing, and downtime, at a leisurely pace. But last night I noticed my to-do list included twelve things (!) that I hadn't gotten to. I also noticed I didn't know what to do with them, because they weren't easily moving onto my new list.

I finally gave up and went to bed without the satisfaction of throwing away the old to-do list, because I had a new one started. The new one was started, alright, but those twelve things were stuck on the old list.

Human beings are unique and complex, and I could probably do a multilayered analysis of my relationship with to-do lists. But this morning, as I looked at those twelve things from yesterday and the new busy day ahead of me, I couldn't help but wonder what they might have to do with being an introvert. And then I decided to take the long hot bath. :-)

Recently I presented a workshop on introversion. One of the handouts featured simple diagrams of the introvert and extrovert brains, showing the main blood pathways. On each of the handouts, I traced the pathways in red marker by hand, to make them easier to see. The extrovert path is a smooth, relatively short trip with one circular loop. The introvert path is longer, more complicated, the kind of road you wouldn't want to take without a map. By the time I finished multiple tracings, the term "busy introvert brain" had a whole new reality for me!

Our introvert brains are designed to enjoy being busy, with ideas, thoughts, impressions, and feelings. We think, we process, and we mull things over. We go deep into our thoughts (and deep into our brains!). In significant ways, we're satisfied experiencing the world internally.

The thing about my to-do lists, a daily ritual for decades, is that I always make them with a real intention of carrying them out. As I think back to making yesterday's, I know I didn't at all plan on having twelve things not done by the end of the day. And after all, I'm no rookie at this. By my calculation, I probably have close to fifteen thousand to-do lists under my belt. My hunch is that I'm operating under a strange and mysterious illusion that my body can operate as fast as my busy brain.

A couple years ago, I had the opportunity to ask Marti Olsen Laney (author of *The Introvert Advantage*) what she considered the cutting edge for herself as an introvert. She said, "I have a million ideas to write about. I just turned sixty—I need to focus on just a few." I don't feel alone with my busy brain. But what about those twelve things on yesterday's to-do list? And what about that tricky illusion?

Being no to-do list rookie, I've figured out, pretty quickly, that the twelve things will meander their way into this week, on their own time-lines. And as I think about yesterday, I suspect one reason I didn't get to them is that I wasn't rushing and trying to squeeze them all in. That's a good thing, probably a sign I'm behaving more like a conscious introvert! Maybe the illusion isn't quite as tricky as it used to be. But best of all, those frustrating twelve things got me into the long hot bath. Such a deal. :-)

End of food for thought, on to a practical idea:

A Practical Idea *for* Introverts *and* Extroverts

This time of year tends to be busy and complex for everybody,
so don't be afraid to treat yourself to your version
of the long hot bath—often.

INTROVERTLY HAPPY

*L*ast night, I had a great time at a birthday party, but not the way I was expecting.

It was a small gathering: the "birthday girl," who was turning fifty-five, and five of her woman friends. We sat in front of the fireplace, and ate soup and bread and birthday cupcakes, and chatted about nothing in particular.

The birthday girl has old friendships with everyone in the group, but the six of us had never spent time together. I knew it was going to be a small gathering, and I didn't know who was coming. This was a party my introvert self could look forward to, and I did—only a few people, a cozy fire on a winter's night, good food (the birthday girl is a great cook), and the possibility of some real conversation.

Here's what I think I was expecting besides good fire and good food: I had it in my head that because it wasn't ten or fifteen or twenty-five people, I'd find myself at ease in this more-intimate group and get immersed in some in-depth conversations with some interesting women.

What actually happened is I quickly remembered that what I like best is having a great conversation with *one* person. A group of six is no small thing! (The generalization about introverts preferring one-to-one interaction isn't an exaggeration.) But what happened after I got clear about that is what I truly wasn't expecting: I had a great time being immersed in small talk!

As I settled myself in, really close to the fire, I began sizing us up. One other guest was a self-identified introvert, and one was an extrovert. I don't know how the other three identify, but my hunch is one introvert and two extroverts. That would make an even balance: half introverts, half extroverts. Now I may have had some help from being so close to the fire—it was *very* relaxing. :-) But what I noticed is that once I realized an in-depth conversation with one person wasn't going to happen, I went with the flow, and I liked it.

Something I learned is that small talk isn't synonymous with superficial. The conversation moved from one thing to the next. Little reports about people's lives, a question here and there, comments about the food, laughing, periodic interruptions to pet the two roaming chocolate labs, a short discussion about a book.

At first, I tried to figure out how to be part of this little group and how to be in the conversation. Maybe it was the fire, maybe I was tired, but I gave up soon and just went with it. The extroverts were being extroverts, setting a lively but not speedy pace. The other introverts seemed

34

comfortable being themselves, listening and talking. As for me, I discovered a way to be with myself and with the group at the same time that was surprisingly pleasurable.

For starters, once I gave in, I realized this party was doing fine with or without my participation. The pressure was off. I was free to do what I felt like. Mostly what I felt like was watching and listening. Five beautiful people were being relaxed and natural and having a good time, and I got to be in their presence.

A topic would come up that I could have added a story to, but the pace was faster than mine, so mostly I'd enjoy my story silently. It was part of the conversation, just not spoken. Same with opinions. I loved hearing what people said about the book, and I added a comment or two, but mainly I enjoyed my own perspective privately and didn't have to generate much energy to keep up with the pack. And when I got tired, I quietly excused myself and went home. They paused to send me off warmly and got right back to business.

The moral of this story, for me? Don't underestimate the potential to be "introvertly" happy in any situation. (And don't cheat yourself on time in front of the fireplace.)

End of food for thought, on to a practical idea:

A PRACTICAL IDEA *for* INTROVERTS *and* EXTROVERTS

The next time you're in a group setting (of any size),
remind yourself that who you are speaks louder than whatever
might come out of your mouth at a given moment.
Then relax and enjoy yourself.

DOING THE
RIGHT THING

*T*his afternoon, I gave myself the choice of a hot bath or a cold walk in the woods. I picked the cold walk. It was a case of "doing the right thing." For four hours, mainly with pencil in hand, I'd been wondering what I could say today about being an introvert, and I had no idea. Frustrated, I decided it was time for some action, literally. Wouldn't you know, by the time I got out the door, I had an idea. I almost turned around and headed for the tub.

My study of qigong has intensified in the past several months, and it's giving me some new thoughts about introverts and action. Ancient Chinese philosophy says that all energy is made up of two forces, called "yin" and "yang." Everything in the universe, including our bodies, has yin and yang energy—they can't exist without each other. (Yin and yang are often illustrated with a circle divided in the middle by an "s" curve, with one half white with a black dot and the other half black with a white dot.)

A bare-bones description of yin energy would say it's internal, passive, spiritual, and female in nature. Yang is external, active, physical, and male. One more important point about yin and yang: they need to be in balance. Out of balance, much can go wrong.

I'm anything but an authority on qigong or the world of yin and yang, but I do trust these basic principles. And I'm clear that, if I have anything to say about it, I'm all for maintaining good yin and yang balance in my body. I've learned enough about yin and yang to understand that it's a very complex subject, but even so, when I look at the descriptions, common sense tells me that introverts predominate with yin. We get our energy from that internal world of thoughts, ideas, feelings, and impressions, and our behavior tends to reflect it.

On the subject of introverts and action, you could say I picked the cold walk in the woods over the hot bath for the sake of my yin-yang balance. And it wasn't an easy choice! Some years ago, when I began to understand the research on temperament and the distinct physical differences between introverts and extroverts, I was particularly struck with (and comforted by) the finding that it's harder for introverts to move our bodies, because we predominate on the side of the nervous system that requires conscious thought. For extroverts, movement happens more easily with less intention.

It was one of those lightbulb moments for me. No wonder I've always loved the part of hiking where you lie down on the ground and look up at the sky—it's because of my parasympathetic nervous system, not laziness!

But in my study of qigong, I'm learning that too much "brain work" creates too much acid in the body and calls for physical action. And walking is very good for people, because we have a point on the bottoms of our feet—in from the ball—that's connected to our kidney energy channel. (And kidney energy is life-force energy, "the most important energy to our life," to quote Master Chunyi Lin.) We energize our life force when we walk!

So what's an introvert to do with a body that's inclined to be yin in a universe that wants it to be yin and yang?! And what's an extrovert to do in a body that's inclined to be yang in a universe that wants it to be yin and yang?

The simple answer, I suppose, is to strive for balance. Introverts should cultivate action. Extroverts should cultivate inaction. For me, the ancient Chinese wisdom and the new scientific research keep me curious and in awe of the mystery of life in the body. (And I managed to squeeze in a hot bath.)

End of food for thought, on to some practical ideas:

A Practical Idea *for* Introverts

Become a brain-overload detector. Train yourself to automatically get up and go for a stroll—around the block, around your office, around the house—whenever you sense your brain getting tired. Don't make a big deal of it. Create a habit: weary brain = time for a walk. Your body will start to like it.

A PRACTICAL IDEA *for* EXTROVERTS

The next time you're alone and feeling bored—about to call somebody, turn on the TV, listen to music, scrub the floor, check your email, and so forth—give yourself permission to sit down for a few minutes and tune into your breath, not meditating, just breathing and doing nothing. Fluff up your yin!

No! No! A Thousand Times, No!!

A few weeks ago, I heard a leadership expert say that the ability to say no is one of the most important skills a person can have. He also happens to be an expert in body language, so he demonstrated the difference between a skillful "no" and an unskillful "no." The skillful no I'd describe as "friendly confidence" body language. I was impressed. Maybe it was "wishful looking" on my part, but it seemed as though if you do it well in your body, everybody can feel almost cheerful that you just said no. It's been on my mind ever since. It was great to get a reminder about the importance of being good at saying no. But what I'm wondering about is the happiness factor—how to get good at being *happy* saying no.

Ellen DeGeneres says in America, we're suffering from TBS: Too Busy Syndrome. Being good at saying no is one remedy for that malady, across the board. Even if we didn't have TBS, it's part of our basic well-being to be good at making choices—saying yes, saying no, opening things up, setting limits. It's when I think of myself as an introvert that the happiness question comes up.

It makes sense for everybody to be skillful at saying no. For introverts, it's essential. For one thing, our energy flows out faster than extroverts', and it takes longer to replenish. (And we need a low-stimulation environment in which to do the replenishing.) Managing our energy well in this overstimulating world means being good at setting limits.

For another, introverts don't get what the researchers call "hap hits" ("hits" of happiness) from being up on the surface. We get pleasure from experiencing things in depth. We like to reflect. We like to be thorough. But we live in a world that operates a lot like channel-surfing. Protecting our depth-seeking selves from too much living in the busy shallows involves saying no.

But back to happiness. It's one thing to be good at saying no. (In fact, the research on temperament gives introverts a high grade for being able to say no to ourselves.) It's another to enjoy it. I notice a difference between saying no to the outside world and saying no to myself. I've grown to often actually enjoy saying no to things I know will overstimulate me, such as a big New Year's Eve party or a networking event, which I've officially given up forever. :-) It's a pleasure to imagine the overstimulation I've avoided.

But setting the more internal limits seems harder and more complicated. Of these generalizations about introverts, I identify with every one: Introverts love to learn. They feel things deeply. They're good at concentrating. They like to think. For me, saying no to a good thought process, a strong feeling, or something new to learn about is hardly ever enjoyable. And because that internal land of the mind is so fluid and not very concrete, in the moment, it can seem like there's room for everything, and the sky's the limit! Not true, of course, because I live in a body (and wear a watch).

Sometimes I say no to myself and feel deprived. Sometimes I don't say no and feel overwhelmed or exhausted. And then there are the times when I find a way to step outside my mind, bless its heart, to look for the yes or no. Sometimes it's by walking, sometimes following my breath, sometimes climbing into the bathtub. However I get there, the answer usually comes pretty easily, and I'm almost always satisfied.

So here's my plan: I'm going to unlock the secret of friendly-confidence body language. I'm going to keep fending off the outside world, with a smile. And I'm going to negotiate more time off for my busy mind. It's no big deal: just say no. :-)

End of food for thought, on to a practical idea:

A Practical Idea *for* Introverts *and* Extroverts

Pick a day to track how many times you say no (to yourself and to others) and for what reasons. Also notice how you feel each time. Reflect on it and take a next step for yourself in the "no" department.

Enough

A few days ago, I came across a quote I'd written on a blue index card some years ago. It says, "So much power in short and sweet!" No source is noted, which is uncharacteristic of me with quotes. I have no memory of where it came from. Maybe I made it up :-)—but I don't think so. I pulled it out from the pile, and I've been staring at it regularly.

Here's a paradox about introverts that makes me smile. We're known as the quieter ones, but give us the right subject at the right time in the right place, and we can talk up a storm. It's as if a button gets pushed, and the rich complexity comes billowing out in all its detail. Sometimes it seems like all or nothing for me. I'm interested in a middle way. I get the idea of the power in short and sweet. Poets are masters at it, creating whole worlds from a few carefully chosen words. Maybe the trick is to become a poet :-)—or at least tap into that poetic sensibility. (I wonder how many extroverts write poems.)

In the last issue of *The Introvert Energizer*—"No! No! A Thousand Times, No!!"—I reported on my pursuit of the happy no. In the spirit of short and sweet, and mostly for the fun of it, here's an update from the front line.

Emma the cat, my daily companion, age nineteen (extreme introvert), doesn't like going outside. But this winter, every so often, I've detected a subtle pull toward the front door from her as she and I come down the stairs and head for the kitchen. I always jump at the chance for Emma to have a little fresh air. At our house, we call it fluffing up the DNA. My job is to slowly open the two doors to the (cold) front porch and hold the outer door open, staying completely still.

If she's still there by that time (a cat of strong constitution but with no tolerance for fast movement), she sits at the doorway, her nostrils sniffing the air. Sometimes she only sits and sniffs. Sometimes she comes through the doorway and sits in the porch, sniffing the colder air coming through the screen door. And sometimes she walks around the porch in a slow circle.

Whatever she chooses, at some point, she finishes fluffing up her DNA and slowly heads back in toward the kitchen. Because I'm frozen as the silent door prop (sometimes pretty literally), I watch her decide how much is enough. It looks deliberate and easy. I want to be like Emma.

End of food for thought, on to some practical ideas:

A PRACTICAL IDEA *for* INTROVERTS

Think of something you have many thoughts and feelings about. Get quiet for a few moments and then write two good sentences about it.

A PRACTICAL IDEA *for* EXTROVERTS

The next time you're with an introvert who's talking up a storm, get curious. Try cheerfully wondering about what makes this person tick.

THE INTROVERT SMILE

'm sitting in a coffee shop, watching a man who's walking around looking at the photographs on the walls. To get a close-up view, he leans over the table of a woman sitting at her laptop until his chin is just inches above her head! My eyebrows rise, wondering what she'll do, but she totally ignores him! (He doesn't stay there long.) I can't help but smile at this scenario—it's got my attention—and the next thing I know, he's at my table, pointing to another picture, asking me if I know which mountain it is. I'd guess he's an extrovert. :-) But what I'm thinking about is my smile.

Some years into discovering myself as an introvert, I must admit it's one of my favorite things in life. I coined the term "conscious introvert," and I love turning myself into one. I see five broad categories: understanding that it's physical to be an introvert; reframing—that being an introvert is an asset; taking good care of that valuable commodity, energy; finding introvert ways of doing things in an extroverted world; and becoming skillful at extroverting when it's called for.

Recognizing introversion as an asset may be the most significant. It makes me happy. Paying attention to my energy is challenging but not optional, and it has its rewards. It's challenging because the world is so busy, and my life is, too. And it's challenging, because no matter how much my body gets drained or overstimulated, my mind has an old habit of trying to ignore it. If I don't pay attention, the cost is too high. But the more I pay attention, the more energy I have, which is a good thing.

Finding introvert ways of doing things (in an extroverted world) is like working on a jigsaw puzzle. Sometimes I'm engrossed, then I forget about it, then something draws me back into the game.

And it's a subtle process. Talking less and enjoying it more is an introvert way of doing things for me. Having fewer expectations for myself to say what I'm thinking or feeling extends not only to extroverted environments but even to ideal introvert situations, such as one-to-one conversations. I'm finding it relaxing.

Getting more skillful at extroverting is less like solving a jigsaw puzzle and more like reading the whole god-blessed manual for my cell phone, hoping it makes a difference. It puts me out of my comfort zone, but it's a good idea. Occasionally I take an extroverting risk and almost never regret it. Being a good small talker is a big extroverting goal of mine. Periodically I practice a little, but mostly I just think about it.

But about smiling. I've got a new category for conscious introverts that I call "introvert/extrovert fusion." And I see the "introvert smile" as an introvert/extrovert fusion strategy. Last fall I learned that smiling stimulates many energy points on the face. Wanting my energy points to be well-stimulated, I've increased my smiling considerably since then. :-)

But let's not underestimate the potential of a good smile! A generalization made about introverts is our tendency to be focused inward. Out in the world, that may happen because we're engrossed in our thoughts and somewhat oblivious to what's going on around us. Or it may be a more deliberate strategy to conserve energy.

In either case, it's quite possible we're not smiling. And it's not hard to see how inward-focused, unsmiling introverts could give rise to assumptions of shyness, unfriendliness, and self-absorption.

Here's where the introvert smile comes in. My definition: an authentic (maybe subtle) smile, sending a message that you're present, available, but not necessarily about to start a conversation. It's extroverting in its outward focus and introverted in the intention to "stay home," a comfortable fusion.

In the coffee shop, I don't know if I was exhibiting an introvert smile or a generic grin. The man and I talked a bit about the mountain, he in sentences, me in one-word responses. It made me happy and didn't use much energy. And I stimulated those energy points!

End of food for thought, on to some practical ideas:

A PRACTICAL IDEA *for* INTROVERTS

Try out the introvert smile.

A PRACTICAL IDEA *for* EXTROVERTS

Be on the lookout for people who seem shy, unfriendly, or self-absorbed and wonder if you're right.

Stewarding Our Energy

A few days ago, I glanced at a calendar and noticed it was the Hindi New Year. Into my mind came one of my Hindu friends. I wanted to call her up to wish her a happy new year, but within a moment of the thought, an "introvert monitor" showed up and canceled the idea. I felt disappointed but resigned.

This friend was out of the country for more than a year, and even though she's been back a few months, I haven't talked to her. I knew I wouldn't be satisfied calling her unless we could have a real conversation. It wasn't that I didn't have enough time—I didn't have enough energy. My tank was empty. As I sat there knowing I wasn't going to call her, I also felt a little resentful, because I could easily think of several extroverts in my life who could make a two- or three-minute "Happy New Year" call, have a great connection, and come away satisfied and no doubt even energized.

51

The Dalai Lama has said the most important thing we can do is to "steward our energy." I've been fascinated ever since I heard it—that one of the most respected spiritual leaders in the world would say managing our energy is the most important thing! I'm fascinated, and I'm trying to figure out how to do it. The Dalai Lama didn't say the most important thing for *introverts* to do is to steward our energy, but I know he wouldn't disagree.

As luck would have it, I'd barely finished being disappointed, resigned, and resentful when I happened on a reading that I'm sure would get the Dalai Lama's stamp of approval. It reminded me that stewarding my energy is probably more about going with my flow and less about figuring it out. And I notice I'm speculating that one of these days, my introvert monitor will give me the go-ahead to call somebody and wish him or her a happy new year without also having a wonderful conversation. It won't take too much energy, I'll be satisfied, and we'll have the wonderful conversation later.

End of food for thought, on to a practical idea, which is the reading I happened upon:

A Practical Idea *for* Introverts *and* Extroverts

"Rest when you're tired. Take a drink of cold water when you're thirsty. Call a friend when you're lonely. Ask God to help when you feel overwhelmed. Many of us have learned how to deprive and neglect ourselves. Many of us have learned to push ourselves hard, when the problem is that we're already pushed too hard. Many of us are afraid the work won't get done if we rest when we're tired. The work will get done; it will be done better than work that emerges from tiredness of soul and spirit. Nurtured, nourished people, who love themselves and care for themselves, are the delight of the Universe. They are well-timed, efficient, and divinely led." —Melody Beattie, *The Language of Letting Go*

Going on Vacation

s you're reading this, I may be scuba diving—and I may not. My sister, brother, and I are on the island of Cozumel, Mexico. My brother fell in love with scuba diving several years ago and has become masterful at it. For at least two years, he's been trying to round up our extended family to go off together and check out diving. So far it hasn't worked. I think he decided to take the bull by the horns and make something happen. In January, he invited my sister and me to go to Cozumel with him for a week in April, and we said yes.

I said yes to Cozumel but not necessarily to scuba diving. Fifteen years ago, I spent a week snorkeling not too far from there, and I loved it. But as a friend put it, identifying with my ambivalence, being that far underwater would be "a stretch" for her. A stretch is right!

Before I understood how introverts are put together, I probably would have been squirming with this dilemma and not feeling very kindly toward myself—wanting to be a good sport, probably defending my right to say no thanks, but secretly labeling myself a party pooper. I'm still squirming, but with compassion.

It's not that introverts and scuba diving don't match. For all I know, introverts are attracted in droves. After all, it's a quiet activity that's not done in crowds, and no small talk is involved. :-) But let's not forget these introvert bodies. In our brains, we have a higher blood flow to the frontal lobes, the area that promotes thinking before acting. And our favorite neurotransmitter is acetylcholine, which has the job of saying, "let's think about it." The acetylcholine pathway is long, and it's known to require overnight processing to store and to retrieve information.

Plus, of the two sides of the autonomic nervous system, we predominate on the parasympathetic, which focuses on slowing down and relaxing. (Extroverts predominate on the other side, the sympathetic, the action side.) So introverts are designed with busy brains that like to think and to reflect about what we're experiencing. A couple weeks ago, an extrovert whose husband is an introvert said to me, "Introverts—lots of depth there." Our nervous systems accommodate our busy brains with a slower pace. Too much stimulation too fast overwhelms the operating system.

We need time to ease into new situations. We enjoy what's familiar. We're fascinated with the world, but we relate to it quite differently than extroverts. It's why we're known as the quieter, more reflective ones who tend to move at a slower pace.

As you read this, I'm more than halfway into my week in Mexico. My busy brain and introvert body have their hands full: the luxury of a whole week with my sister and brother. My rusty, fledging Spanish in a world of Spanish speakers. Pesos. Snorkeling. Tropical island life after a winter of snow banks. (And sleeping in a strange bed!) If I *am* scuba diving, I'm glad I'm being watched over by an expert who loves me, because if I meet a shark, I'll probably have to think about it.

End of food for thought, on to some practical ideas:

A PRACTICAL IDEA *for* INTROVERTS

Remember to love yourself up when you're in unfamiliar territory, even a new restaurant.

A PRACTICAL IDEA *for* EXTROVERTS

Compare notes with an introvert in your life about sleeping in an unfamiliar bed.

"Feel the Fear and Do It Anyway"

I went scuba diving. In the last issue of *The Introvert Energizer*, I predicted that I might, while on vacation in Cozumel with my sister and brother. Not wanting to cause undue suspense about my prediction, I'm reporting in. :-)

My ambivalence about scuba diving is no doubt multifaceted. For instance, I grew up on the prairie. The closest lake was ten miles away, and a swimming pool was nowhere near, so I spent little time in water. Because I'm endlessly curious about life as an introvert, my preparation for Cozumel, and the possibility of scuba diving, included an "introvert analysis." I knew I'd be dealing with lots of unfamiliarity, a common challenge for introverts. I knew my slower introvert pace would love a week of relaxation and unscheduled time. And I wondered whether all the stimulation I'd get on this trip would be more than enough for my introvert self without adding something as exotic as scuba diving. So I decided I'd only try diving if I felt like it. It wasn't going to be one of those scary but worthwhile challenges.

By the morning of our second full day in Cozumel, I'd gotten back into the swing of snorkeling (fifteen years after my first experience). And my expert diver brother was painting such a relaxing picture of a beginner dive that I felt like doing it, so I said yes. He made arrangements for the next afternoon. I spent that day pleasantly unconcerned about my upcoming adventure. But by night, fear hit. And there I was with a scary (but worthwhile?) challenge in my lap.

What to do? After patiently enduring a lot of dissecting of my inner landscape as we sat in the balmy night air, my sister and brother finally said good night. I squirmed with indecision: to dive or not to dive. Finally, I thought back to the morning, when I had agreed to go. My decision had felt so right. I decided to trust it. The dive was on, but so was the fear.

A book I'm fond of from the 1980s—*Feel the Fear and Do It Anyway,* by Susan Jeffers—didn't come to mind, but I suspect it's in my bones enough to have helped me out. What I like most about this book is the way it normalizes fear. Among its "five truths about fear": "The fear will never go away as long as I continue to grow"; and "the only way to get rid of the fear of doing something is to go out and do it."

So I took the direction of "determined and afraid." I didn't sleep very well that night, and the next day I was mainly preoccupied with being afraid (but determined) right up to dive time, 3:00 p.m.

A conscious introvert, as I say, does five things: (1) understands that it's physical to be an introvert; (2) reframes—being an introvert is an asset; (3) takes good care of his or her energy; (4) finds introvert ways of doing things in an extroverted world; and (5) becomes skillful at extroverting when it's called for.

I'd say my baby scuba dive is an example of extroverting. I use "extroverting" as a word to describe introverts doing things that are more natural for extroverts. Extrovert bodies are designed to work more comfortably with the external world and with the unfamiliar in the external world.

To gain entrance to that exotic (and beautiful) underwater world of the ocean, I got numerous instructions from our dive master, on land: several ways to equalize the pressure in my ears, sinuses, and lungs; strategies for dealing with my mouthpiece (the lifeline to air!) if it came out in the water; how to maneuver the tangle of hoses that were coming with me; plus a short course on diver sign language. Then I had to pass the competency tests—underwater! (Enough said.)

But even though this was challenging extroverting for me, I think I found, or was given, an introvert way to do it, thanks in large part to my sister's and brother's, introverts themselves, being so understanding and accommodating of my need to talk it through. (Fortunately or unfortunately, my sister had a cold that exempted her from her own scuba process.) And thanks to my brother holding my hand, literally, as we made our way twenty-five feet under the water.

A few days ago, he e-mailed me a little video clip the dive master took. There I am, not quite like a deer in the headlights, but close. But my brother is holding my hand, and all is well. (And I'm glad I went diving.) End of food for thought, on to some practical ideas:

A Practical Idea *for* Introverts

Think of some extroverting that's interesting but scary and fantasize about getting support to do it.

A Practical Idea *for* Extroverts

Think of some introverting that's interesting but scary and fantasize about getting support to do it.

WHERE'S THE DOWNTIME?!

*S*unday night, I got out my calendar to see what the week looked like and got a little nervous. It looked busy, just like last week. It wasn't a shock—I'm the one who fills up my calendar—but there I was, facing the music. I'd had a couple weeks' worth of more stimulation than usual, including quite a bit of extroverting, and I had maybe more than a couple weeks to come, peeking ahead. So I wondered where in the heck I was going to get some downtime here (a basic necessity for us introverts).

I went to bed without an answer. But Monday afternoon, I found myself taking a walk, actually a stroll, in the woods instead of staying at my desk. The freedom of self-employment. :-) I noticed I was watching the warblers intently, not out of the corner of my eye. And I was stopping to gaze at the beds of little wild violets, not out of the corner of my eye.

I had a little insight there on the trail. In fact, I sat down to have it. I remembered how easy it was in my twenties, as a pretty avid bird-watcher, to spend hours birding. It wasn't a strong enough passion to hold its own once I became a mother. But I'm a lover of the natural world, and in my heart I still consider myself a "birder." Maybe in a sort of introvert way, I'd decided it didn't matter so much that I wasn't birding anymore, because I had the experience inside me.

Here's the insight: I realized there's a big difference between knowing how to do something or remembering something and actually doing it. Knowing you can ride a bike because you did it constantly as a kid isn't the same as riding the bike. That thought is a no-brainer. :-) What makes it an insight is that I could feel it in my body. It was as if my internal "introvert analyzer" put two and two together and said, "Hey, you need to get out more—smell those roses!" And I got it!

Yesterday, toward the middle of my packed day, I found myself, a little defiantly, grabbing my knitting bag and deciding to knit two rows on my dishcloth, even though I supposedly "didn't have time." (I'm not a real knitter, but I like the feeling of making dishcloths, so I do it in spurts.) And I had another insight, another no-brainer, but I felt it in my body—that I could seize the moment and have a little fun, literally for a couple minutes. So I did.

(And I remembered a book I like but haven't looked at for years. It's called *20-Minute Retreats—Revive Your Spirits in Just Minutes a Day with Simple Self-led Exercises*, by Rachel Harris. It's full of ideas that take fewer than twenty minutes, in case seizing the moment interests you.)

Where's the Downtime?!

This might be Insight Week, because last night I started having another one about downtime. I think it underlies "get out and smell the roses" and "seize the moment—have a little fun." The insight is that downtime means giving the brain a chance to rest. Another no-brainer, on the surface. What I'm getting in my body is that rest means *rest*.

But the brain's "resting" is mysterious. I know that if it were completely resting, I'd be dead. I know it's on duty 24/7—but sleep experts know brains do rest during sleep, even if they don't understand it very well. Researchers have figured out introverts need to sleep after receiving input, because our information and experience get stored into long-term memory while we sleep. ("Sleep on it" is a good habit for introverts.) The body's resting, but the brain's working—and resting at the same time?!

I tend to read and reread descriptions of the blood pathways of introvert and extrovert brains. I find them fascinating and complicated. When I see the longer, more-complicated introvert path and read about how busy it is, I can get tired just thinking about it! But what do I mean, I wonder, when I say that downtime means giving the brain a chance to rest? Where *is* the rest in downtime?

I think I've been "collapsing" solitude and downtime. My particular busy introvert brain (and body) likes a lot of solitude. I use solitude for lots of things. But when it comes to producing overstimulation, my brain can beat Disneyland hands down. And I can do it really well in a low-stimulation environment, all by myself. Solitude doesn't guarantee downtime in my world.

What I think I'm getting this week, in my body, is that for me, downtime means something like "being in the moment with my senses," giving my honorable, hard-working, complicated introvert brain a rest from thinking, by smelling the flowers, working with my hands, or staring out the window at a cloud. It's a state of mind: not thinking while doing *or* not doing something. I like hours of it at a time, but I'll take it in minutes, too.

End of food for thought, on to some practical ideas:

A Practical Idea *for* Introverts

Take a look at how you give your brain a rest from thinking.

A Practical Idea *for* Extroverts

Compare notes with an introvert in your life about how you relax.

WORKING HAPPILY EVER AFTER

Recently an *Introvert Energizer* reader suggested I write about possible careers for introverts. I've been thinking about it. Ten years ago, not particularly aware of myself as an introvert, I bumped into an ideal job (for an introvert like me). I recognized it almost instantly, seized the moment, and have never regretted it. After forty years in the work world, these ten years of extreme satisfaction are very noticeable to me.

Thinking about introverts and career, I decided to look at my own work to see what makes it a good job for an introvert. Here's what I notice. (I help introverts have a great life: life at its best, no matter what the challenges, as my slogan goes. I do it through life coaching.)

I get to set my own schedule, an advantage if you're looking to take good care of your energy. I work almost entirely one to one, in a quiet, mainly undisturbed atmosphere, which includes a twenty-year-old introvert cat and a young extrovert dog. :-)

Introverts tend to be good listeners, good observers, and good at focusing, and we don't like small talk. My work is essentially the opposite of small talk and is full of listening, observing, and focusing.

Introverts like to learn. Coaching is about learning. Introverts like depth. Coaching is an in-depth partnership relationship that works with outer and inner life, that natural introvert domain. Introverts tend to have high self-awareness. My work is about increasing self-awareness and putting it to good use.

Introverts tend to be creative and to "think outside the box." Coaching is a cross-disciplinary field that's built on one-of-a-kind relationships between client and coach. Because I work with my clients weekly, I have good time to process and to integrate what's happening in their lives. It feels like a comfortable introvert pace. And introverts tend to be independent; my work suits my independent nature. No wonder I'm so happy!

So what are good careers for introverts? Obviously, work that aligns with natural introvert tendencies is good for introverts. But human beings are complex, and so is the world. Passion, curiosity, necessity, and fate lead us to unlikely places. Diane Sawyer, the television anchorwoman, for instance, is often cited as an introvert in a seemingly extrovert role, which makes me hesitant to do too much career compartmentalizing in terms of temperament.

I feel fortunate that in the days before I turned into a conscious introvert, I was able to recognize a good thing when I saw it. Maybe the trick is to keep asking, "What makes me happy?" (introverts and extroverts alike) and go for it however we can.

End of food for thought, on to some practical ideas:

SOME PRACTICAL IDEAS *for* INTROVERTS

Find a way to talk to a young introvert in your life about being an introvert (and why it's a good thing).

Think about what makes you happy at work.

Fantasize about what your new career would be if you changed it.

A PRACTICAL IDEA *for* EXTROVERTS

Ask an introvert in your life what makes him or her happy at work.

INTROVERT
GRANDMOTHER

The day before yesterday, I officially joined the grand-mothers' club! My first grandchild, known these past many months as "Baby JJ" (her parents' first names start with "J"), came out and got her new name, Skylar Jane. I started wondering about being an introvert grandmother last December, the day we got the news about Baby JJ's upcoming arrival. I started wondering, because my family made comments about what I think might be described as my "subdued" response.

It was cheerful commenting. And I suppose because they're so used to my talking about introverts, they even decided it was an introvert way to respond. For me, of course, how I responded was just how I responded. I was in shock. Not that newlyweds announcing they're having a baby is shocking information, but getting the news that you're going to be a grandmother is a shock, of sorts. :-) And I was in awe that a new precious little family member was in our midst.

I do think they were right. I responded like an introvert. Introverts tend to have a slower pace than extroverts. Our longer brain pathways need more processing time than extroverts'. Often we don't talk about what we're thinking. When we get new input, we're clearer about our thoughts and feelings after sleeping on them. We like to reflect on things. And we tend to speak softly. So I had fireworks going on when I found out about Baby JJ, but they were inside.

Over the months of her incubating, I noticed that when people asked me how I was doing with becoming a grandmother, I didn't have much to report. It's as if the grandmother in me had been incubating like Baby JJ. I don't know whether that's because I'm an introvert, but it probably is. Introverts like to know a lot about what we experience. We like depth. It's a little hard to have much perspective on being a grandmother before your grandchild is out and about, giving you legitimacy. :-)

Now Baby JJ has finished incubating, and now I'm a real grandmother. And I'm still an introvert, which makes me an introvert grandmother. I wonder how I'll behave. I already have one of those tiny photo albums that's easy to carry around with you. But it was a gift from an extrovert. :-) I probably wouldn't have bought it myself.

Over the past several years, as I've watched more of my peers becoming grandmothers, I can tell it's a powerful club I've joined. The criterion for membership may be grandchildren, but the main activity is love. I'm glad I got to join.

End of food for thought, on to a practical idea:

A PRACTICAL IDEA *for* INTROVERTS *and* EXTROVERTS

Wonder whether your grandmothers are/were introverts or extroverts and think about how their love comes/came through.

THE CARE AND FEEDING
OF INTROVERTS

A couple weeks ago, I was having a solitary supper, eating a subway sandwich about twice as long as I needed and starting a book I've been curious about for awhile: *French Women Don't Get Fat*. At the back of my mind, I was wondering what I'd write for *The Introvert Energizer* and hoping that reading the first chapter about French women would cancel out half my subway.

The activity at the back of my mind—worrying about overeating, wondering about my writing—was fruitful. I suddenly remembered that Marti Olsen Laney, in *The Introvert Advantage*, says a lot about the care and feeding of introverts. Time for a revisit to see what I might notice, I thought.

In the meantime, I'd turned into an introvert grandmother, so I wrote about that instead. But now, halfway into the secrets of French women, I'm still thinking about introverts and food.

When I learned about the physiology of temperament—that it's literally a physical experience to be an introvert or an extrovert—at first my mind was boggled. It hadn't occurred to me that my vague identity as an introvert (I thought about it essentially never) would have anything to do with how my body works.

When I first read *The Introvert Advantage,* I was trying to understand the information about the brain and nervous system. I was having a paradigm shift: introvert and extrovert *brains*?! By the time I got to the chapter about food, I was on information overload. I read it, but it didn't stay with me. Some time later, I heard Laney speak. One of the things she said, with conviction, is that it's very important for introverts to take the supplement lecithin to build the neurotransmitter acetylcholine.

(Acetylcholine is the key neurotransmitter introverts use on our dominant blood pathways in the brain. It triggers our ability to focus and to concentrate deeply for long periods. It helps us feel calm and alert. The temperament researchers say that keeping the acetylcholine level strong is essential for introverts.)

Laney's matter-of-fact conviction about lecithin got my attention. I did a little research, decided it was reasonable and doable, and have been taking it daily ever since. But will there be an introvert cookbook?! Reading *French Women Don't Get Fat* is the latest example of my participation in the American sport of Figure Out Food (And Keep Eating!). I think it's a game I'll be able to play as long as I want.

In that spirit, here's a nutshell of things I find useful as I revisit what Laney offers from her research:

Our brains and our neurotransmitters—and our bodies—are affected by things like food, exercise, stress levels, and rest. It's a good idea for introverts—and extroverts, too, of course—to get support from food. Foods that are known to help increase acetylcholine are fish (such as salmon, mackerel, sardines, and others), egg yolks, wheat germ, liver, meat, milk, cheese, broccoli, cabbage, and cauliflower.

Introverts tend toward low blood sugar. Eating slow-releasing carbohydrates (the ones that don't make your blood sugar spike) helps maintain optimal blood-sugar levels. It also helps produce another neurotransmitter, serotonin, which promotes calm. Dopamine, the main neurotransmitter for extroverts, increases alertness and makes us feel less hungry. It's created by eating protein. Eating smaller amounts of lean protein throughout the day helps maintain alertness.

And one small secret from the French women: evidently they don't read while eating. A lovely idea I'll keep in mind. :-)

End of food for thought, on to some practical ideas:

A PRACTICAL IDEA *for* INTROVERTS

Think about taking the supplement lecithin.

A PRACTICAL IDEA *for* EXTROVERTS

Ask an introvert in your life how he or she is doing with acetylcholine production. (Just kidding.)

WRITE ON!

I think I'm a happier introvert since I started writing this newsletter. I'm a little surprised to say that, especially because I don't find it easy. But I think it's true. I've never had an aspiration to be a writer. I do have an English degree. I think I got it out of my love for the written word. Maybe it was the closest I could get to majoring in reading. :-) (Reading has always been one of my basic necessities.)

But all those papers an English major has to write were like punishment. No matter what the topic, it felt like "the everything and the nothing." There was everything to say, which was too much, or there was nothing, which was not enough. Halfway in between was not fun. Journal writing is much the same for me. I've done it off and on for decades, but it's another version of all or nothing. The part of me that likes to be thorough can go on forever. But that's a hopeless cause, and my hand gets tired. Often I write nothing in my journal for long stretches at a time.

Writing letters is better. Once I get going on a letter, I still have the urge to say "everything," but it's more pleasurable than writing in the journal (and no comparison to writing an English paper). I think it's the relationship I have with the person I'm writing to that makes the difference. It gives me focus.

But here's what I'm noticing about being a happier introvert. In the past several years, since I've made it my business to find out what makes us introverts tick, I've developed a lot of respect for our challenging brains. They give us a run for our money! They thrive on complexity. Compliments of the way we use the parasympathetic nervous system, introvert bodies are designed to let our busy brains focus and concentrate deeply for long periods, which makes them feel alert and happy.

Our bodies know how to shut out stimulation, because we have so much going on in the front of our brains, where complex thinking happens. We walk around observing, wondering, making comparisons, thinking, feeling, contemplating, and mulling things over. Our brains are very busy, and they like being that way.

And we like words. But the way the introvert brain works means that we tend to choose our words carefully. And it takes time for us to translate the complexity we experience into language. In the practical everyday world of communicating, writing is a good tool for introverts. Writing a note—or even a letter!—or sending an e-mail allows our characteristic thoughtfulness to come out in a way that may feel easier than speaking. More time to choose the right words.

I don't presume to really understand what's going on in my brain. But

I'm starting to suspect it likes this writing work I give it. Twice a month, to produce this newsletter, my busy brain and I sit down to see what we can come up with. It's not easy work. It's more of that busyness: mulling, remembering, wondering, and contemplating.

But there's something about the challenge of finding a focus and then some clarity—enough clarity from within that inner complexity to transform into some words—that my brain appreciates. I can tell, because for a day or so after the newsletter is done, it's as if my busy brain and I get to sleep in, and when we get up, there's nothing to do but lie in our hammocks. If only it would last. :-)

End of food for thought, on to some practical ideas:

A PRACTICAL IDEA *for* INTROVERTS

If you notice a sense of dread about something you want or need to communicate, check to see if you could do it in writing. If you can, go ahead—and feel fine about it.

A PRACTICAL IDEA *for* EXTROVERTS

Don't be afraid to ask questions of the introverts in your life. We're busy trying to manage our brain activity. :-) Sometimes a question is welcome relief!

Introvert Small Talk

Here's what I'm wondering about these days: is there an "introvert way" to make small talk? My daughter, an introvert, thinks she learned how to make small talk from one of her best friends, an extreme extrovert. I have a hunch she's right. The two of them have spent countless hours together over the past twelve years, and my daughter is good at it.

I don't think that happens automatically, though. I'm not good at it, and I've spent countless hours in the company of extroverts myself, over many more years than twelve. I don't hate small talk, but I'm not drawn to it, and I'm not good at it. The word that first comes to my mind about small talk is "boring." But I have a feeling that response is a combination of compensation for my sense of inadequacy, some simplistic assumptions about communication, and good old introvert arrogance.

I'm reading a book about small talk. It's full of tips and suggestions that make sense but aren't inspiring me. It's taking the edge off my simplistic assumptions and introvert arrogance, though. :-) The author says that small talk clears the way for more intimate conversation and that it's a way to acknowledge another person as being "very real and there." I buy that, and it makes me like the *idea* of small talk better. But I'm wondering what it would take for me to like *doing* it.

A stereotype about introverts is that we don't like small talk. That might even be what I call a "respectful generalization" about us. We prefer the meaty conversation, what the small-talk book calls "big talk." If you've been reading this newsletter for awhile, you've heard me say this in one way or another about many things: what can we do—we've got these introvert brains!! They like the big talk.

But I'd like to think I can cultivate a fresh start with making small talk. And I think it has to be "introvert" small talk. Here's the recipe I'm coming up with to try out: it starts with the assumption that small talk is actually important. It includes lots of smiling, something we inward-focused introverts can forget to do, even though we know how. :-)

Introverts are known to be good observers and good listeners. My recipe relies on these basic strengths. The volume is low, and the pace isn't rushed. And although introverts are often encouraged to come up with things to talk about ahead of time when they know they're going into small-talk territory, my recipe leaves that step out—it just seems like too much work. Last but not least, though, I'm giving myself full permission to take breaks into the solitude of the bathroom or the back porch.

But here's what's striking me most: maybe there isn't any real difference between small talk and big talk. Maybe what matters is whether we're "acknowledging each other as being very real and there," and what we talk about is secondary. That is an idea I could get behind.

End of food for thought, on to some practical ideas:

A PRACTICAL IDEA *for* INTROVERTS

Imagine yourself as a big fan of small talk—and
being really good at it.

A PRACTICAL IDEA *for* EXTROVERTS

Imagine yourself at a party, in a corner having
a long, meaty conversation.

DRAINED BY JOY

I missed the last deadline for *The Introvert Energizer*. It came shortly after I got home from a four-day wedding, and I was recuperating from being drained by joy. The wedding was one of those experiences that defy easy description. As a friend of mine said, hearing a short-version report, "Wow, it sounds like a movie!" I agreed. And I wish you all could have been there or at least have seen the movie. :-)

It's not a new experience for me to be drained by joy. Maybe a third of me likes the phrase "drained by joy." The rest of me thinks it's a contradiction in terms and a flimsy attempt to make feeling wiped out sound good.

Here's a snapshot of the wedding, from the "drainee's" perspective: the setting for this four-day event was the shore of Lake Superior, in northern Minnesota. People in Minnesota love, and even revere, Lake Superior, commonly called "The North Shore." I'm certainly a member of that group. The lake was one of my "drainers," so I came home and looked it up on the Internet.

Here are a few good sentences from the U.S. Environmental Protection Agency Web site: "The Great Lakes—Superior, Michigan, Huron, Erie, and Ontario—are a dominant part of the physical and cultural heritage of North America. Shared with Canada and spanning more than 750 miles (1200 kilometers) from west to east, these vast inland freshwater seas have provided water for consumption, transportation, power, recreation, and a host of other uses.

"The Great Lakes are the largest surface freshwater system on the Earth. Only the polar ice caps contain more fresh water. . . . Lake Superior is the largest in terms of volume. It is also the deepest and coldest of the five. Most of the Superior basin is forested, with little agriculture because of a cool climate and poor soils. The forests and sparse population result in relatively few pollutants entering Lake Superior, except through airborne transport."

From where I live, you jump in the car, drive a few hours north (five in this case), and there it is: big, rugged, pristine beauty. By itself, under the right (quiet) conditions, Lake Superior gives me joy, and it doesn't drain me. But these weren't quiet conditions, and they weren't simple. For one thing, it was four days. I know that weddings in some cultures go several days, but what I'm used to is more like a few hours. My introvert self knew ahead of time that a wedding that lasted days would be draining.

The wedding celebration would take place in three locations: the early afternoon ceremony, with 125 guests, under a canopy right on the

shore of the lake (that feels like an ocean). Music and refreshments after the ceremony up the hill in a large white tent on the big lawn of the
log-cabin resort. Then, through the resort woods and across the road to
dinner and dancing in the town hall of the tiny rural village closest to the
resort. Virtually everyone attending this wedding would travel a minimum of several hours.

Family and friends of the wedding couple began gathering on day
one to form a crew that would transform the three sites into wedding
mode. One family was Irish East Coast extroverts; the other was small-
town Wisconsin introverts, interesting to ponder in itself. And there was
a pack of miscellaneous urban Minnesota friends, which included me.

In the way a common goal can do it, we wedding workers turned
into a little community over the four days. We hauled chairs and tables,
folded 140 moss-green cloth napkins into a fancy banquet design, strung
lights on trees, and set up banners and direction signs all over the wedding territory. We spread out tables full of driftwood and beautiful Lake
Superior rocks for the "resident artist" to decorate the dinner tables with.
We helped unload the caterer's van, and we carried big stones from the
lakeshore to make cairns (ancient Irish markers) down by the ceremony
tent. We prepared an outdoor rehearsal dinner for fifty and hosted a post-
wedding breakfast for the wedding guests.

All the while, the wedding couple fed us box lunches, made evening campfires, took us on hikes into the wilderness, and kept us moving with a remarkable set of spreadsheet to-do lists and a lot of light-
hearted flexibility.

But what about my being drained by joy? To digress briefly to discuss a few key traits of introverts: Our brains are designed to be busy thinking about and processing what we experience, so we can get overstimulated by too many experiences in a short time. Unlike extroverts, whose bodies are actually energized by lots of stimulation, introverts get drained and need significant downtime in a low-stimulation environment to process and to get recharged. Creating energy takes more time for introverts, and it flows out faster.

We tend to be observant, thorough, and detail-oriented, and we like depth and meaning. And because of how our nervous systems work, our pace is slower, we tend to be hesitant in unfamiliar situations, and it's harder for us to move our bodies than it is for extroverts.

So this was a situation designed to drain an introvert: driving five hours into the wilderness (with homemade rehearsal dinner baked beans for fifty in the back seat) to spend four busy days, stationed in an unfamiliar log cabin, interacting with between 25 and 130 interesting people essentially nonstop (including offering a toast at the dinner, for added anxiety).

And there was very little of the ordinary about this wedding. Besides that it took place at the shore of the largest freshwater lake in the world, far from everyone's home, this was the marriage of two gay men.

The ceremony was very personal, carefully designed by the two grooms and filled with beauty: a professional a cappella vocal ensemble of friends, live instrumental music, poetry and personal sharing read by friends and family, including the couple's teenage son. And the wedding couple, beaming in their elegant wedding suits. After the ceremony, all the guests climbed out onto the mammoth boulders on the shore for a group wedding picture. A bald eagle showed up to circle above the big white tent as we had refreshments on the lawn. And the town hall was a night of good dinner, good music, laughter, and dancing.

So I was drained by joy. By the time I climbed into my log-cabin bed that night—with day four still ahead of me—I knew I wouldn't have a good night's sleep. My mind was entertaining me with a multimedia slideshow of images and impressions and thoughts and feelings that I put on pause only with great effort, so I could rest for a few hours. And it kept playing for days afterward. The moral of the story? Being drained by joy is worth it, but don't forget to recuperate.

End of food for thought, on to some practical ideas:

A PRACTICAL IDEA *for* INTROVERTS

Think of three things that help you recuperate
from being drained.

A PRACTICAL IDEA *for* EXTROVERTS

Have sympathy for the introverts in your life when
you suspect they're getting drained.

"Slow Down and Feel the Energy"

I’ve been thinking about energy a lot the past few weeks. Last October, I went on a six-day qigong retreat, and this year I did it again. Qigong (pronounced "chee-gung") is Chinese and translates loosely as energy work. It's considered the great-grandfather of all Eastern healing and martial arts and has been around for thousands of years. During the retreat, I effortlessly memorized one sentence from the hours and hours of talks given by the qigong master, Chunyi Lin. It wasn't the title of this article, but close: "You are loved; slow down and feel the energy."

"Slow down" has seemed like a good idea to me for decades. I can remember feeling rushed and too busy when I was fifteen. A mere thirty-eight years later, I took my first serious slowing-down action when I resigned from a more-than-fulltime job and started my life coaching business. Life coaches are known for promoting good life balance, so I was glad that circumstances (plus some determination on my part) were allowing me to put my money where my mouth was. Several years into my coaching business, I started to learn about the physical makeup of introverts, and the idea of slowing down took on a whole new life.

The introvert body is designed to move at a slower pace than the extrovert body because of how our nervous systems are set up to work with those long introvert brain pathways, those busy, thoughtful introvert brains. So it was normal for me to be slower. I decided it was my *job* to slow down! It was not an easy job but one I was up for.

That qigong retreat sentence—"You are loved; slow down and feel the energy"—caught my attention. It stayed in my head, and I found myself smiling when I thought about it. The "slow down" in the middle was, of course, familiar, but in a new context, surrounded by "you are loved" and "feel the energy." I liked it, and I was intrigued.

Master Lin frequently says that energy can be neither created nor destroyed but that it can be transformed. He often makes reference to Albert Einstein as the first one to establish that principle in the Western scientific tradition. In the world of qigong, feeling the energy, the qi ("chee") is the name of the game. In qigong, qi is synonymous with "universal energy" or "life-force energy." In the six days of the retreat, we spent hours every day tracking down and making friends, if possible, with our life-force energy. The instruction was always to go as slow as we could.

"Slow down and feel the energy" is the way to do business in qigong. I imagine that's true across the countless different qigong forms in the world. For an introvert on a mission to slow down, a qigong retreat is a good place, especially if you don't mind tracking the elusive qi, which by definition makes up and flows through everything in the universe.

In truth, the "you are loved" section of my memorized sentence made it stand out. I don't presume to understand this, and it may be inaccurate besides, but what I gather from my study of qigong, and of Spring Forest Qigong in particular, is that life-force energy in its pure form could be called unconditional love. Maybe my sentence boils down to the idea that love is everywhere, and the trick is to feel it.

I think of my favorite Einstein anecdote. Someone asked him, "What's the most important question?" And he answered (not the exact quote), "The most important question is: 'Is the universe friendly?'" These days, home from qigong land and back in the regular world, my sentence still makes me smile. I'm working on slowing down and feeling the energy. And I think the answer is yes, the universe is friendly.

End of food for thought, on to a practical idea:

A PRACTICAL IDEA *for* INTROVERTS *and* EXTROVERTS

Memorize this sentence—if you haven't already :-)—"You are loved; slow down and feel the energy." And check it out.

QUIET LEADERSHIP

A couple months ago, I heard about a book called *Quiet Leadership,* by David Rock. My first thought was, "Hmmm, a book for introverts." Now I'm reading it, and a week or so ago, when it was time to write the next *Introvert Energizer*, I thought, "Hmmm, maybe this is what I'll write about." But I didn't. Instead I got distracted, drained, and paralyzed. I boiled it down to that just this afternoon, shuffling through the dead leaves on a walk in the woods, tired and frustrated and making myself walk.

The good news is that once I boiled it down, I quit feeling frustrated and stopped being paralyzed. I'm still somewhat distracted and drained but managing fine. And I'm finally writing this newsletter. :-)

I'm drained, because I've had a lot of extroverting in the past couple weeks and not enough downtime. I'm distracted, because I'm about to start studying some new material that has my intellectual self wanting to

89

disappear for a couple months, with no interruptions. I dipped into it, and it's taking up a lot of space in my head. And I was paralyzed, because once I started chewing on quiet leadership, I decided I'd have nothing to say about it without a PhD (in something or other).

Of course, versions of distracted, drained, and paralyzed are normal for introverts. Our brains and nervous systems are designed to really like thinking, wondering, and concentrating on things we're interested in. We get what the brain researchers call "hap hits" ("hits" of happiness) for doing it. No wonder I let myself get prematurely distracted by some deep thoughts. It feels great! And we live in a very extroverted society, which seems to be stuck in overdrive. Our introvert bodies get deenergized by the external world, no matter how much we love it. It's no small thing to find the right balance of being in it and retreating to get our neurotransmitters restocked. Drained batteries are an introvert fact of life.

About the paralysis: As I understand Jung, who coined the terms "introvert" and "extravert" early in the twentieth century, and people who interpret his work, if extroverts orient themselves by connecting to the outer world of people, places, and things, introverts orient ourselves by connecting to the inner world of archetypes—not just our own inner worlds, but the inner world of what Jung called the "collective unconscious," or the "reservoir of our experiences as a species," as one psychology scholar describes it.

This is deep-thought territory, of course, and I won't say much more. But when I stop to imagine the possibility that, indeed, our energies are directed by this vast field called the collective unconscious and that we're swimming around in that field, sizing up our thoughts and feelings in relation to what's going on out there in the "real" world, I have even more respect for the introvert tendency to be thoughtful.

And even more compassion for us as we go at our slower pace, pausing before we take action, because we're doing the work of deciding whether the action makes sense against that huge backdrop of the collective unconscious.

But back to *Quiet Leadership*. I've decided to skip the PhD and to say a few things anyway. :-) For one, it's true that it *is* a book for introverts, but not in the way I first assumed. (I thought it would be about a style that's quiet.) The subtitle is "Help People Think Better—Don't Tell Them What to Do!" It's an approach to leadership that's about helping people improve the way they think, based on the latest brain research, which is interesting for introverts and extroverts alike. As I'm reading about this model, my hunch is that it's well-suited to introverts. We like to think, so, by nature, we're probably attracted to the idea of getting better at it. And we tend to be good listeners, so a model of encouraging better thinking probably works well for good listeners.

But beyond David Rock's work, I'm liking the term "quiet leadership." It has a calming effect on me and makes me want to think deep thoughts. :-)

And I recommend shuffling through dead leaves even when you're really tired.

End of food for thought, on to a practical idea:

A PRACTICAL IDEA *for* INTROVERTS *and* EXTROVERTS

Lie down for three minutes, or as long as you want! Get quiet, go inside, and imagine yourself tuning into the collective unconscious. As the theory goes, we all have it in us. Introverts just relate to it more intensely.

"This Is the Time for Introverts!"

A couple weeks ago, I got an e-mail from an *Introvert Energizer* subscriber who said, "I think now is the time for introverts. . . . Now that we have an introvert for a president-elect, I'm eager to see how he taps into his inner resources to steer our nation in the best direction that he knows to be true. I'm willing to bet he'll go against popular grain more than once, because he's listened to and acted upon his inner convictions. He also is a fan of Lincoln, one of the most famous introverts. . . ." I haven't heard that President-elect Obama identifies himself as an introvert, but he certainly seems to fit the profile.

Here's a quote from an interview he did with the *Chicago Sun-Times* in 2004: "The biggest challenge, I think, is always maintaining your moral compass. Those are the conversations I'm having internally. I'm measuring my actions against that inner voice that for me is audible, is active.

93

It tells me where I think I'm on track and where I'm off track."

Here's my current list of key strengths of introverts:

- Strong ability to focus and to concentrate deeply

- Tendency to be good observers, good listeners, good planners

- Tendency to be very responsible

- Tendency to be independent and to have the strength to make unpopular decisions

- Tendency to be studious, smart, creative, flexible

- Ability to recognize the complexity and vastness of a subject and able to understand how change will impact everyone involved

- Tendency to be cooperative

- Especially effective one to one

- Able to set a slower pace

From what I can tell, I'd say Obama qualifies.

Five years ago, when my fascination with temperament started, it wasn't long before I developed a conviction about introverts and the world—that our extroverted culture is longing for more "introvert energy," more quiet, more reflection, a slower pace. And because the United States has been such a noticeable extrovert in the world, if we created a dynamic introvert/extrovert balance in our national character, the whole world would benefit. (See my Web site—www.introvertenergy.com/introvertswow.php—for a bit of visioning about an introvert-friendly world.)

So I'm looking forward to our new (introvert) president's term with curiosity. If we're talking change, I'm guessing the introverts of the world would get behind better introvert/extrovert balance in a heartbeat. (It might happen without legislation!) And if President-elect Obama is, indeed, an introvert, I wish him an unlimited supply of presidential downtime.

End of food for thought, on to some practical ideas:

A Practical Idea *for* Introverts

Look at that list of key strengths of introverts above. Pick three to appreciate about yourself and embrace them even more.

A Practical Idea *for* Extroverts

Look at the list of key strengths of introverts and choose three you'd like to see more of in the world. Cultivate them in yourself, if you wish, and appreciate them in others.

BATHTUB READING

I started out the new year in the bathtub, reading a magazine article about fungi. It was a long interview of Paul Stamets, a fungi expert, about his book, *Mycelium Running: How Mushrooms Can Help Save the World*. I read the whole thing in one sitting, so to speak. :-) It made me very happy. For one thing, the article was well written. For another, I'm now fascinated with the subject of fungi and impressed with Stamets's expertise and commitment. And I think he's probably right: mushrooms can help save the world, especially if Stamets keeps helping the mushrooms. Last but not least, reading the whole thing all at once felt like a small miracle.

I've been wanting to read this article for eleven months. I know that because the magazine, *The Sun,* arrived last February. *The Sun* always has an in-depth interview, and I read most of them. Usually these interviews wait patiently for a couple months before I get around to them. And I almost never give myself the luxury of reading the whole article at once. But this one waited the longest (so far!). In fact, I think my bath on New Year's morning was a spontaneous now-or-never, because I've almost recycled this issue several times.

New Year's morning, it either caught my eye or came into my mind—I don't remember which—and I seized the moment. I told myself it was a holiday, bypassed my usual process of figuring out what to read, and climbed into the tub with it. What took me so long?! And why did I like it so much when I finally read it? It's not hard for me to find "introvert" reasons.

Introverts tend to be studious. Our minds feel really alert when we're learning, thinking, and wondering about things. We like depth, and we're good at concentrating when we're interested in something. But we can get overstimulated and drained—brain overload. Being interrupted is unpleasant for us, and getting our concentration back can take a lot of energy. It takes time to think and to ponder, and time to get our brains out of overload when the neurotransmitters get depleted. And even after we've learned a lot about something, chances are we'll feel like there's still so much more to know and to think about.

I could tell I wanted to read about mycelium when I first skimmed the article last winter, even though it's been more than forty years since I studied chemistry or biology, and even though I didn't think I'd ever heard of mycelium (which is not true, I'm sure). But every time I sat down with it, I'd get interrupted, and, true to introvert form, it did take too much energy to jump back into a subject I was so rusty in.

I understand it when Stamets says both animals and fungi inhale oxygen and exhale carbon dioxide, suggesting that humans are more closely related to fungi than we are to plants. But if I got interrupted there, I couldn't pick it up days later and resume at the section about fungi stomachs. I'd have to start over, which got old fast. On New Year's morning, though, when I finally got to the end of the interview, I had the same reaction as the interviewer: "Stamets fundamentally changed my view of nature. . . ." I didn't just get some interesting information about fungi. It shifted my paradigm, and in an expansive way, providing a very satisfying learning experience.

Of course, now my introvert brain wants to think about this idea of fungi helping save the world. What to do? Reread the article? I don't have a photographic memory, and I read it on New Year's Day in the bathtub (holiday reading), so I didn't even underline. To have a decent conversation about it, I'd need to read it again. Or should I give in to my curiosity and get the book? A fundamental shift in my view of nature is no small thing, certainly worthy of one book, to a book addict like me. And it's not satisfying to leave something this interesting at one article. After all, I just found out mycelia use the same neurotransmitters humans use to think! The hunger for depth isn't easy to ignore.

Besides "the pleasure of finding things out" (the title of a collection of short works by Nobel physicist Richard Feynman, no doubt an introvert), there's also the issue of being an informed citizen. Some months ago, I read an article in *The Atlantic* called "Is Google Making Us Stupid?" My story about taking a year to read a seven-page article would fit right in. But piles of books and articles hover around me, and it takes energy to bring a new body of information into my head—and energy is a precious introvert commodity.

What to do? Here's what I know: I love to read, and I love open-ended thinking, and I'm not doing enough of either. I don't know if I'll get the book or reread the article. But I'm glad the mycelia are out there doing their amazing mycelium business, and I'm trusting that if Google is making us stupid, it's only temporary.

End of food for thought, on to some practical ideas:

A PRACTICAL IDEA *for* INTROVERTS

Look at your reading life: are you satisfied with it? If you are, have a moment of smiling. If you're not, how can you make it better?

A PRACTICAL IDEA *for* EXTROVERTS

Compare notes with an introvert in your life about your reading likes and your reading habits. And what about Google's influence? Has the Internet changed your reading life? How?

Introvert Response Ability

It's the day after Obama's inauguration, and I'm hanging out in the afterglow. I woke up this morning with the phrase "a new era of responsibility" from the inaugural address going through my mind. I think President Obama said, "It's time for a new era of responsibility." Yesterday I wasn't thinking this, but today I am: I wonder how many of those two million people on the Mall at the inauguration were introverts, and I wonder how they're doing today.

I joined the inauguration festivities last weekend via TV, starting with the presidential train ride into Washington, D.C. It's been years since I've seen this much TV. Once I got into it, I wasn't completely mesmerized, but almost. I watched the inauguration ceremony itself on the big screen, with a crowd at a neighborhood theater. And last night I spent an hour and a half in another crowd, a happy, noisy inauguration party organized by friends, in a neighborhood restaurant. Today it feels almost like I was on the Mall yesterday. I'm wiped out.

The day before the inauguration, on *The Oprah Winfrey Show*, I saw a clip of a film I believe the actress Demi Moore is directing. The clip was of celebrities, it seemed (although I recognized only some), making pledges, one after another. One guy pledged to think of himself as American instead of African American. Somebody else pledged to remember to turn off the lights more often. Some of the pledges, like those, were personal, practical. Others, as I recall, had broader scope and were more like projects.

I can't remember this film project's name—it's a work in progress—but I gathered it's aimed at encouraging people to participate in helping the world work better. Maybe it's an early sign of the new era of responsibility. This afternoon, in my inauguration afterglow, I remembered those pledgers with a smile—they inspired me—and I decided to make my own pledge.

I may be premature in announcing it. I haven't slept on it or even thought about it much since I got the idea (a few minutes ago). But it's not inconsistent with my general tendency, so I'm trusting my intuition and going for it. :-) My pledge is to be more of an introvert.

Now, many people in my life would say I have a strong—some might even say exaggerated—sense of responsibility. It's a common introvert tendency, and I do have it. It's probably not surprising that I woke up this morning with "a new era of responsibility" in my head. I'm so responsible that some people in my life might even prefer a new era of *ir*responsibility for me.

But today I'm thinking about responsibility as "ability to respond." I'm wondering about my pledge this way: what's my ability to respond to the world even more as an introvert? I like the question. It's too soon to have a good answer, of course, but I think it has to do with slowing down even more, being even quieter and more thoughtful—and feeling happy to do it. As my saying goes, "The world needs more introvert energy!"

End of food for thought, on to some practical ideas:

A PRACTICAL IDEA *for* INTROVERTS

Join the movement! Pledge to be more of an introvert. :-)

A PRACTICAL IDEA *for* EXTROVERTS

Pledge to be more of an extrovert. What would that look like?

SPOTTING
INTROVERTS

t's not that easy to spot an introvert. I say that, because an *Introvert Energizer* reader recently pointed it out to me. She wrote in response to my suggestion, a couple issues back, that the Nobel physicist Richard Feynman was an introvert. I have a superficial knowledge of Feynman from a book of his I haven't read yet. I glibly assumed that someone with his depth of focus, an introvert trait, would be an introvert. This writer, knowledgeable about Feynman, corrected my assumption and pointed me in the direction of information about him that certainly paints the picture of an extrovert. And it makes me even more interested in reading his book.

I have several introvert friends who tell me people have a hard time believing they're introverts. I periodically get that reaction myself. Of course, knowing whether somebody's an introvert or an extrovert isn't a particularly hot topic. No doubt everybody knows those two words and has at least a vague notion of what they mean. But it works not to know very much, because it's not a main way we identify ourselves.

Essentially, almost since the psychoanalyst Carl Jung coined the terms "introvert" and "extravert" early in the twentieth century, introverts have had a bad rap. And American society is very extroverted. Until recently, research has suggested that the ratio of extroverts to introverts is three to one. So from an introvert's perspective, it may be just as well that we aren't routinely identified. Not my point of view, but a possibility. :-)

The research about how the brain works is changing the way we think about lots of things, including introversion and extroversion. According to temperament research, based on our genetics, we're born with a personal "set point" on the continuum between extreme introversion and extreme extroversion. Our set point is the place where we function best.

Philosophers and scientists have speculated about people's tendencies to be inwardly or outwardly focused for many centuries, long before Jung presented his theory and coined the terms "introvert" and "extravert." But now science has documented that introverts and extroverts are a physical reality. It's not just an attitude or a state of mind.

As I've written in previous issues, those introvert/extrovert set points have to do with how our brains and nervous systems work. Introvert bodies are designed to function best with inward focus, and extrovert bodies with the focus outward. Introverts get energized when we're focusing inward on thoughts, ideas, and impressions, and we feel drained when there's too much attention outward. For extroverts, it's the reverse—they're most comfortable focusing on people and things.

But what's my point? Well . . . it's not that easy to spot an introvert. After all, introversion may be a physical trait, but the brain and nervous system are invisible. Plus, we're on a continuum—lots of variation possible. Additionally, introverts don't have a choice about focusing on the outer world (behaving like an extrovert). It comes with being in a body. If we've got a lot of energy stored up, we may even be acting like an extrovert because it feels fine. We may even be *trying* to be an extrovert, because it's easier to fit in that way. Plus, human beings are complex and multifaceted. It's easy to make wrong assumptions.

I think my underlying point is that spotting introverts is a good thing, including spotting ourselves as introverts. A few months ago, I attended a gathering where I had many opportunities to talk about my work, which involves coaching introverts. I was struck with how often people asked questions aimed at wondering whether they were introverts. I wasn't expecting that much uncertainty, and it's not uncommon for people to think they're extroverted and introverted, depending on the situation. But the research suggests that, just as with being left- or right-handed, everyone tends toward one side or the other of the continuum.

I think spotting introverts is a good thing, because our culture is long overdue on tapping into the potential of the gifts introverts have to offer. Think quieter, slower, more thoughtfulness, for starters. And spotting introverts is a good thing to do, because being an introvert is no small challenge in the twenty-first century. The more conscious we are of temperament, the better we can work with the challenge. I'm all for making it a hot topic.

End of food for thought, on to a practical idea:

A Practical Idea *for* Introverts *and* Extroverts

Talk to someone you haven't before about whether he or she is an introvert or an extrovert. Find a way to have the conversation.

"Ask Without Hesitation..."

A few days ago, I was in a coffee shop that's not my regular hangout, staring at the huge menu board above me. When the woman behind the counter asked what I wanted, what came out of my mouth was, "Decisions, decisions, decisions." She said, "Yeah, I heard a report on public radio that too many choices causes stress." I think I read about that research myself awhile back. It makes sense.

These days I'm carrying around two sayings, given to me by friends, both extroverts. One goes, "Ask without hesitation, give without depletion." The other is, "How can I make it easy?" Some time ago, I wrote about the Dalai Lama's saying the most important thing we can do is to "steward our energy." I think he could have added "and it's a fulltime job."

I have compassion for introverts and extroverts alike in the face of all the information we process, all the stuff we interact with, and all the decisions we make. As an introvert, though, I notice I'm feeling impatient lately. I'm trying to steward my (precious) energy, and it's not easy.

I once heard Marti Olsen Laney (author of *The Introvert Advantage*) describe the introvert body as the kind that's designed to be sitting in a cell, working on old manuscripts. Introvert minds feel very alert wondering, looking into things, going in depth at an unhurried pace. I like the image of quiet monks. But these days it seems like the monks are so busy picking the size, shape, color, and bristle-type of their toothbrushes, it's hard to get at the old manuscripts.

Here's another complaint: let's say I do have an old manuscript, and I'm sitting in my cell with it. I might have an introvert brain, with its ability to focus and to concentrate deeply for long periods of time, but I've got it programmed to feel guilty about doing that. I've trained myself to feel in a hurry. It's a busy, complex world, not oriented to introverts, and I'm in the middle of it, coping. Complaining aside, I'm going for being a happy, relaxed monk—in street clothes :-)—so I'm grateful to have these two sayings. These days I'm carrying them around on a little pink slip for easy reference.

Introvert brains are natural planners, so I like to think I'm training mine to *plan* on making things easy, just by posing the question a lot: how can I make this easy?! Even if I can't or won't come up with an answer on the spot, the question is worth asking.

I think of the phrase "Ask without hesitation, give without depletion" as a soothing balm. In this busy, complex world, it reminds me to conserve my precious introvert energy and to trust that partly how it happens is by being willing to receive.

End of food for thought, on to some practical ideas:

A Practical Idea *for* Introverts

Make a "pink slip" to help you remember to be good to yourself.

A Practical Idea *for* Extroverts

If you have some compassion available, extend it to an introvert in your life by remembering that what gives you energy—people, places, things—drains her or him.

DEEP BUDDY

<hr>

Ten days ago, I lost a deep buddy. My friend Mark Lindblad died unexpectedly of a massive heart attack. He was fifty-five. "Deep buddy" isn't a term I use often. In fact, maybe it's brand new to me, but it's what comes out of my mouth when I talk about Mark's death.

Mark and I were initially colleagues. We met about ten years ago. As one of the many people grappling with the shock of losing him, I'm thinking about him and our friendship a lot. This morning, wondering what leads me to call Mark my deep buddy, I realized I'm confused about whether he was really an extrovert. I'm pretty sure we've talked about it. And over the years, watching his ease in a group and having some sense of the breadth of his personal connections, I'd have to assume he was. But when I think of Mark as my friend, I'm a little confused about it.

Introverts and extroverts tend to have different definitions of friendship. Someone an introvert considers an acquaintance, an extrovert very possibly would call a friend. Introverts tend to have fewer friends than extroverts, and we probably expect our friendships to be deeper and more "meaningful" than extroverts do. I do meet the introvert criteria that way.

Mark and I didn't connect regularly. Weeks or months might go by. But over the years, we periodically spent hours and even days together, in various processes connected with our work, and the processes weren't superficial. And over the years, we had occasion to give each other support about things going on in our lives, so our relationship had the gift of time.

I remember being somewhat overwhelmed with Mark's presence when I first knew him. He was a big, tall guy, and very friendly, even forceful—probably an extrovert who stood out in a crowd. :-) But early on, I realized he was meeting me where I was at. His energy seemed to quiet down to a level I was comfortable with when he was with me. He was a master of playful seriousness and serious playfulness, often happening at the same time. He seemed to focus with ease. And wherever he focused, he brought his full attention.

I also experienced him as a master of positive regard. He seemed to meet life with a combination of curiosity, awe, and love. He always seemed fascinated. And whether Mark and I were in a group together or by ourselves, I felt the impact of his way of being in the world. It was noticeable.

So I've lost my deep buddy, Mark. And I think I'm part of a crowd.

End of food for thought, on to a practical idea:

A PRACTICAL IDEA *for* INTROVERTS *and* EXTROVERTS

Give some attention to friendship in your life. Wonder about it and maybe do something to keep it satisfying.

Nowhere to Go, Nothing to Do

'm on retreat, day five of seven, in the middle of five hundred acres of virgin forest on the coast of South Carolina. I hear the ocean in the background. I wrote an issue of *The Introvert Energizer* the last time I was here, more than a year and a half ago. I'd brought eighteen books along, and I was thinking about me and books. This time, I'm thinking about open-ended time. (And I brought only eight books, FYI.)

This is a spiritual retreat center, but it has no program and no prescribed activities, so there's no shortage of open-ended time. On the sill of the window I'm sitting at, a lime-greenish gecko about six inches long, including three inches of tail, is sunning itself in the open-ended time.

The night I arrived, I was preoccupied with getting settled, but by morning, I noticed I was literally excited about not knowing what I was going to do. It was almost an activity in itself, knowing there was nothing

I had to do and not knowing what would happen next. Besides the luxury of being in what I experience as a profoundly spiritual atmosphere—five hundred acres, no less :-)—I'd have to say this lifestyle of open-ended time is my favorite thing.

I don't know that it has anything to do with being an introvert. These days, I'm reading about the brain and leadership, a new field brain researchers are calling "the neuroscience of leadership." One of its findings is that organisms (including people) like autonomy, "the sensation of having choices." The more we have, the less threatened we feel. I'd guess extroverts like autonomy as much as introverts, so we're probably all attracted to open-ended time. It seems to evoke autonomy. This week, not only do I have lots of autonomy, but it includes the choice of doing pretty much nothing, as often as I want.

That first morning, once I got into the flow of the open-endedness, I probably couldn't have been happier, slowly making some breakfast, doing a little lunch prep on the side, reading a few pages here, a few pages there, figuring out what to put on after my pajamas, getting clear about the day right as it was happening, slowly. The icing on my cake this week, by the way, is solitude. It isn't constant, but it's abundant. And I get to choose it!

If both introverts and extroverts like having open-ended time, we probably part company when it comes to how we use it. (And it certainly wouldn't surprise me if the concept of retreat comes from an introvert.)

So here I am, an introvert on retreat, with full permission to flaunt my introversion. :-) Slower pace. Quieter presence. Natural absorption in my thoughts. Speaking only when I feel I have something to say, or deciding not to say anything, even if I do. Not getting drained, because I'm going at my more natural pace, plus getting plenty of downtime. Having a real conversation with someone when the opportunity arises. And enjoying the complexity of my thought process without having to draw any major conclusions (for now). For an introvert, being on retreat could be a way of life!

Mostly I haven't been ruminating about this pleasurable experience of open-ended time. But if it's as universally appealing as I suspect, I do wonder what the world would look like if we *ran* on open-ended time. In the meantime, the gecko and I are clocking our hours. I think it's ahead.

End of food for thought, on to a practical idea:

A Practical Idea *for* Introverts *and* Extroverts

In the next four weeks, carve out a period of open-ended time,
from sunrise to sunset, and see what you notice.

DIVING DEEP AND SURFACING

The phrase "diving deep and surfacing" came into my mind a few days ago. I think it may be the title of a book. I know it's not original to me, and I have a feeling I didn't read it if it is a book. But I'm definitely identifying with the idea, and I'm not surprised. If breadth is a concept associated with extroverts, the parallel for introverts is depth. And the surfacing makes natural sense, especially if you've ever actually dived!

Here are a few wandering things I have to say about myself and diving deep. It's so satisfying to be thorough, to go deep, that I almost can't help it. What if I *can't* help it?! Sometimes I'd love to dive into something, but I hesitate, or even decide not to, because I'm afraid I may forget to surface and pay too big a price—or not forget, but choose not to, and still pay a big price. (And *not* diving has its own price.)

116

I notice that my deep diving can drive extroverts around me crazy.

Some things in life are optional, some aren't. How do I balance choosing what attracts me with what one of my clients calls "do-outs," things that *must* be done? Especially when I almost can't help but dive deep, no matter where I am? It seems like a deep diver could use up all his or her oxygen on just the do-outs. For me, diving deep, interestingly similar to my one real scuba diving experience, is comprehensive. It impacts me physically, mentally, emotionally—and probably spiritually, but I'd have to think more about that.

Not to bore you with a long list, but here's what comes to mind as I randomly consider places I'm diving or have dived recently: Some special spring presents for my nieces. Writing an article for a professional newsletter. Emma the (elderly) Cat having kidney issues. Getting obedience-trained with Frances the Corgi. Four days of qigong conference. Multiple books I'm reading. Being a good mother. Turning into a grandmother. Becoming a laptop-computer user. Coaching each of my clients, precious, fascinating. Being in all my relationships, really. And planting flowers. I could go on. :-)

My own experience of diving, which I don't assume is universal to introverts (but it may be), is that the depth seems potentially endless. The question of when to come up for air isn't a small one. Satisfying as it is, I notice diving deep and surfacing aren't light exercise. And they take time. And they don't respond well to rushing.

I've been in this introvert body for quite some time now, so I'm not a beginning deep diver. But being conscious of it as part of my introverted temperament is relatively new. This week, I'm trying to cultivate a little amusement at the meaningfulness of it all. I think becoming a master gardener can wait until my next lifetime. And I'm going shopping for a raft.

End of food for thought, on to a practical idea:

A Practical Idea *for* Introverts

Wonder about you and diving deep—and surfacing. :-)

A Practical Idea *for* Extroverts

The next time you're frustrated with someone who seems to be taking too long, being too thorough, or attending to too many details (this very well may be an introvert, whether you know it or not), imagine him or her dressed for a scuba dive.

Six Years
of Introvert Bliss

few days ago, I realized *The Introvert Energizer* is two years old this month. That got me looking back on the past six years of my (happy) preoccupation with being an introvert. Six years ago, I found out about the hardwiring of introverts and extroverts. It made a big impact on me. I went from oblivious about being an introvert to fascinated. But more important, I got a remarkable sense of relief. It came on fast and hasn't gone away.

I'm not disinterested in biology, but it's not one of my favorite subjects. I was a little surprised that the neurobiological research on temperament was so compelling. But as I began to understand how the introvert/extrovert differences in brain blood pathways and neurotransmitters and autonomic nervous systems make such a difference in daily life, I wasn't bored.

And as those of you who've been reading this ezine for some time have probably noticed, what started as relief soon translated into happiness. I was relieved to find such good, concrete reasons for my lifelong experience of so often seeming to be going "up the down staircase" in our extroverted culture. I think my happiness comes from understanding that nothing was wrong with me after all, but also from getting to know what a fine model of human being the introvert species is, and from life's getting more satisfying as I've turned myself into what I call a "conscious introvert."

In my armchair analysis of the world, it wasn't long before I was theorizing that life would be better for everybody if these concrete and complex differences between introverts and extroverts were more widely recognized. And not only recognition—I became interested in the possibility of things changing, of the world working in a way that, overall, suits introverts and extroverts better. That won't be a small change. Who knows what it'll take?

Six years ago, Marti Olsen Laney's book on the physiology of introversion, *The Introvert Advantage—How to Thrive in an Extrovert World*, seemed about the only resource focused exclusively on introversion. Since then, she's written two more (including one on introverts and extroverts). I'm currently reading another guide for introverts, published last year, called *Introvert Power—Why Your Inner Life Is Your Hidden Strength*, by Laurie Helgoe. And I notice a book called *The Introverted Leader*, by Jennifer Kahnweiler, has just come out, as have several other recent titles about introverts. Looks like awareness is growing.

Six years into my own conscious introversion, it seems more natural than ever to me. And I watch my clients feeling more at ease and more skillful in negotiating their way in an extroverted world. In the two years of writing this ezine, I've received messages from many places in the world, mostly about how challenging, even painful, it is to be an introvert. It makes me wonder whether the whole planet is due for a shift. Boiled way down, and understated, what I see as the introvert contribution is a slower pace, a quieter way, and more thoughtfulness. I don't think Planet Earth would mind. :-)

These days, there's less clarity about how many introverts there are. *The Introvert Advantage* proposes the ratio of three extroverts to every introvert, a statistic that's been used for some time. But two recent MBTI (Myers-Briggs Type Indicator) population studies put introverts in the majority! Helgoe's book is based on that assumption.

I remain curious. In my reading of Laney's work, it's not clear whether her numbers come only from MBTI sources or also from the brain research. And if more introverts are being born, what does that say? If the numbers were never accurate and there have always been more introverts than extroverts, what does *that* say?! In the meantime, I love being a conscious introvert.

End of food for thought, on to some practical ideas:

A Practical Idea *for* Introverts

Name three things that make you happy to be an introvert.

A Practical Idea *for* Extroverts

Ask an introvert in your life what he or she likes
about being an introvert.

Around the World in Eighty Hours

little over two weeks ago, I came home from a three-week pilgrimage to India. It seems I can't tell the story of this trip without introducing a dimension of life in my body that's an interesting subtopic in the conversation about introversion, which is that I'm a "highly sensitive" introvert. High sensitivity, of course, isn't just a subtopic. According to research, it's a trait shared by 15 to 20 percent of the population of all mammals, not just people. It's of particular interest for introverts, because statistics suggest that 70 percent of highly sensitive people (HSPs) are introverts. Some years ago, when I interviewed a couple dozen introverts for a writing project, a fair number talked about their high sensitivity and considered it intertwined with being an introvert.

Elaine Aron, author of *The Highly Sensitive Person* and a number of other books about high sensitivity, is the research psychologist responsible for raising consciousness about this trait. Like introversion and extroversion, high sensitivity is a physical characteristic: "a highly receptive, highly sensitive nervous system . . . designed to notice subtleties in the environment."

Back to me and my trip to India in my highly sensitive introvert body. I bring up high sensitivity in talking about India, because it seems such a potent ingredient in the experience. Comparing high sensitivity and introversion to see what can be said isn't a small undertaking, and I hope someone is doing that. What I'll say here intuitively (most of my coaching clients turn out to be highly sensitive introverts) is that being highly sensitive as an introvert seems to turn up the volume. It's maybe a more intense version of life as an introvert.

So, about going to India. This wasn't my first trip; it was my seventh. But it had been seven and a half years since I last went. Here's the moral of this story, I think: I'm glad to be a conscious introvert (and a somewhat conscious HSP). Seven and a half years ago, I didn't identify as an introvert or highly sensitive. I like it much better this new way.

I'd guess probably no one who visits India from the West (and my hunch is this includes people who were raised in India) would disagree that it's very highly stimulating to the senses. The density of people. The easy possibility of cows, goats, dogs, chickens, boars, and burros mingling freely with the humans. The indescribable traffic patterns. Activity seemingly twenty-four hours a day. Breathtakingly beautiful color wherever you turn. The way the harshness of deep poverty intermingles with all other modes of living. Sadly, more and more pollution.

And depth and richness of culture that, to me, feel palpable. India is, of course, a very old culture. A scholar friend of mine who's lived in India for several decades was talking to me about India and continuity. He said the information Indian culture has about its past is astonishing. People know what people were eating for breakfast in India five thousand years ago. He laughingly told me about an Indian "hit tune." It's a mantra Indians today sing with the same words and melody as they did eleven thousand years ago! It's an old culture and a culture whose ground of being is spiritual.

For a highly sensitive introvert like me, going to India could be the kind of activity her mother would strongly discourage. :-) Besides that it's dramatically overstimulating, we were on the road thirty-nine hours going and forty coming back, nonstop extroverting through eleven time zones. Add to that the dimension of pilgrimage, that this was a spiritual journey as well as a physical one, and we have an experience that boggles my heart and mind and is always hard on my body. But I think I'll do it again as soon as possible.

Even before I identified consciously as an introvert, I'd guess I was doing a fairly good job of taking care of myself while in India, or I wouldn't have gone six times. What I regularly say about the benefits of being a conscious introvert is that you have more of the four "Es": energy, ease, effectiveness, and enjoyment. I was happy to notice that was true for me on this trip. There's a cheerfulness I've developed about the challenges of being an introvert (and highly sensitive) that made this trip more matter-of-fact than any I remember. I think it comes from how much I've grown to *love* being an introvert.

I took more vitamins than usual and found a special "travel tonic" to help prevent airplane-induced maladies. I did get sick a couple days after we arrived. It seems to be part of my pilgrimages. I think of it as part over-stimulation, part spiritual cleansing. But I didn't resist it—much. And I appreciated that my symptoms were gentle and that being mildly sick gave me a lot of downtime I probably would have otherwise skimped on.

I gave myself permission, for the first time, to do very little social-izing, somewhat challenging, because I was surrounded by interesting people from all over the world. But I don't regret it. I made it a point to write every day. Usually it was sort of feverish scribbling to describe the day's events, with a little of my thoughts and feelings sprinkled in. On the one hand, that was frustrating. I was having rich experiences and only enough time or energy for "the facts." But on the other hand, I liked it. I knew I was saying enough to get me back into my impressions later. I have eighty-six (little) journal pages I'm really appreciating these days.

While I was sick, I prescribed qigong walking for myself. Those of you who've read *The Introvert Energizer* for awhile know I'm a student of qigong ("chee-gung"), an ancient Chinese field of energy work. Qigong teaches that walking is very good for our life-force energy, our kidney en-ergy, because it stimulates kidney points on the balls of our feet. Walking is also great for helping busy introvert brains move that brain energy down into the whole body. I could often be seen bundled up, slowly walking the verandahs, plugged into my iPod—such a fun way to recuperate. :-)

To our pleasant surprise, my traveling companions and I discovered we'd been upgraded to business class when we got to the Mumbai airport to board our 2:30 a.m. flight to London. My highly sensitive introvert body got to stretch out under a nice quilt in the quite-empty business-class section and rest luxuriously for almost ten hours—a little present from the universe to help me rejoin the masses in the coach section through two more flights to Minneapolis.

Once home, I felt not one bit guilty having a whole week with nothing on my schedule but rest and reentry (a habit I got into a few India trips back, which used to include guilt). The following week, last week, I noticed I felt more focused and rested than ever by that time, post-India. The highly sensitive introvert back home, bright-eyed and bushy-tailed— pretty much.

End of food for thought, on to some practical ideas:

A Practical Idea *for* Introverts

Think of something new to do to take care of your introvert self the next time you travel.

A Practical Idea *for* Extroverts

Smile at all those solemn-looking, inward-focused introverts next time you're cooped up with them on a plane. :-)

"She's Very Ingoing!"

'm in the middle of creating a talk (working title: Love Those Introverts!), so I've been doing homework. I came across a reference to introverts as "ingoing." In the United States, of course, we're very familiar with the word "outgoing." In fact it's the preferred way to be.

The more I thought about it, a few days ago, the more it seemed "outgoing" and "ingoing" could almost be stand-ins for "extrovert" and "introvert." Extroverts focus out. Introverts focus in. It's way more complex than that, of course. But I was liking the simple clarity. Some of us are outgoing, and some of us are ingoing.

Today I'm in the library, so I decided to look in a real dictionary, as opposed to Dictionary.com, bless its heart. I asked where the big dictionaries are, because the one I usually use wasn't in its stand. The librarian took me to a shelf and pointed out what he called the monster, which is the twenty-volume *Oxford English Dictionary* (plus three volumes of "new work in progress"). And he showed me the two-volume Oxford, also a monster by my standards.

I give you all these dictionary details, because I'm realizing this is a little story about "ingoing." The truth is, although I'm a lover of words, I've never taken the time to make friends with a dictionary. In my mid-twenties, I got a big *American Heritage Dictionary* for my birthday one year, and I bet it was my favorite present. I still use it all the time. When the librarian pointed out that long row of the twenty-volume monster (and the volumes are all hefty), my first response was shock. But almost immediately I felt a little thrill, the kind I get when I walk into a bookstore.

I've trained myself to be very focused in bookstores. I almost never browse. If I let myself follow my natural inclination, as a hopeless lover of books, I'd be there when the store closed, busily being ingoing. I saw that twenty-volume dictionary (including the three smaller "new-work-in-progress" addendums) and thought, "Wow!!" Luckily, it was way over my head, and the two-volume baby monster was right at eye level, so I picked it, a little reluctantly, but knowing that a mere quick peek at the big monster would be even more disappointing. As it was, I had to tear myself away from the two-volume book. It was twice as big as the one I usually use on the stand and made me want to make friends with a dictionary, even maybe my old *American Heritage*.

Here's what I found about ingoing and outgoing: between 1930 and 1960, a new definition of outgoing emerged: "Extrovert, sociable, open-hearted, friendly." The timing makes sense, because Jung coined the terms "extravert" and "introvert" in the 1920s.

I was, of course, not surprised to find no comparable definition of ingoing from that time. Here's one for ingoing that showed up between 1920 and 1929, though: "penetrating, thorough." I can identify.

Of course, just because the two-volume *Oxford English Dictionary* doesn't have a nice definition of ingoing that matches the outgoing one doesn't mean it shouldn't be there. And who knows, maybe the twenty-volume edition explains all about it, that it's missing only because there isn't enough consciousness about the importance of ingoing as a way of being yet. In the meantime, maybe I'll let myself sit down with one of those "new-work-in-progress" addendums one of these days, just for the fun of it.

End of food for thought, on to some practical ideas:

A PRACTICAL IDEA *for* INTROVERTS

Say to yourself, "I'm very ingoing!" a few times, like you're bragging, and see what you notice. :-)

A PRACTICAL IDEA *for* EXTROVERTS

Think of an introvert in your life and say to yourself, in an admiring way, "Wow, she's [or he's] so ingoing!" and see what you notice. :-)

INTROVERT/EXTROVERT FUSION

A few weeks ago, I had an interesting morning that included my longest-ever sustained experience of introvert/extrovert fusion. "Introvert/extrovert fusion" is a term I coined for strategies that combine elements of introverting and extroverting. I've written about what I call the "introvert smile," for instance. I define it as an authentic, maybe subtle, smile that sends a message that you're present, available, but not necessarily about to start a conversation. It's extroverting in its outward focus and introverted in the intention to "stay home," a comfortable fusion—and a good way to dispel the myth that introverts are shy, unfriendly, or self-absorbed.

But my interesting morning wasn't a strategy. It was a whole experience that just happened, and it was remarkably comfortable. The setting was an early-morning workshop: two leaders and maybe ten participants, counting me. It started with informal gathering time, refreshments. The format of the workshop was a warm-up activity followed by short presentations of material interspersed with discussion, about two hours' worth by the time I headed out the door.

The introvert/extrovert fusion experience was so compelling that it's what I was thinking about as I drove away. I thought to myself, "Hmm. It felt like I was introverting and extroverting at the same time!" Not a familiar feeling. (In my fascination with introverts, more often than not, I'm watching myself, with a running commentary on how things are going for me the introvert.)

Usually I compartmentalize. I gear up to go to a birthday party and think of it as extroverting. I come home from an eight-hour meeting and remind myself I'm overstimulated by all that extroverting to help me (hopefully) carve out extra downtime. Or I have a day of open-ended time by myself and think how much my introvert self appreciates it. Compartments: introverting and extroverting. But this was different. It didn't seem like I'd been extroverting. I felt very much myself, an introvert in a comfortable mode. Although I was extroverting, it seemed more natural than usual, almost no big deal. And I the introvert was definitely leading. I wondered how it happened.

Here's what I came up with. Almost everyone was new to me in this group. One participant I'd been in a similar setting with once or twice, and one of the leaders is my friend and a colleague. She happens to be a very conscious introvert. So for one thing, having a conscious introvert I know and love in charge of this gathering automatically created a level of comfort. And it offset the efforts of making small talk with a group of strangers at 7:15 in the morning!

Because she's such a conscious introvert, my co-leader friend made a reference to introverts and extroverts in the introduction. When the group debriefed on the warm-up exercise, which involved fast mingling and coming up with quick answers, it wasn't hard for me to identify myself as an introvert and to report that the pace was challenging.

The other leader is an extrovert. Although she didn't identify herself that way, it was obvious. :-) I could tell that the two of them attend to their way of co-leading. I don't know that they specifically think of themselves as an introvert/extrovert team, but by my standards, they demonstrated good introvert/extrovert fusion.

The material they presented wasn't superficial, and neither were the group discussions. My introvert brain was stimulated, and I found myself contributing at my own pace, including at one point explaining that I was going to say something about a topic we'd already finished, because I'd needed a little more time to think about it.

What's the moral of this story? I'm not sure. But before I speculate, let me digress a moment to review whom I consider to be a conscious introvert, because I've been referring to my friend, the workshop co-leader, that way. "Conscious introvert" is the term I use to describe an introvert who knows about the recent information on the physicality of temperament, that our bodies are hard-wired to be introverted or extroverted. And a conscious introvert is aware that our society tends to be very extroverted.

A conscious introvert also reframes his or her perspective on introverts, believing that it's an asset, not a burden, despite numerous negative misconceptions in the world at large. He or she takes good care of his or her energy, which is no small task in a world that's not introvert-friendly. And a conscious introvert cultivates his or her own introvert way of life and develops the extroverting skills he or she wants or needs. My friend the co-leader completely fits the bill.

The moral of this story may be that one conscious introvert leader can create an introvert-friendly environment without even trying. Or maybe it's this: "Don't be afraid to compartmentalize. There are better days ahead." :-) Whatever the moral, I'm a fan of introvert/extrovert fusion. And I think it's time for me to brush up on my introvert smile—it's been awhile.

End of food for thought, on to some practical ideas:

A PRACTICAL IDEA *for* INTROVERTS

If you haven't uncovered your introvert smile, give it a try. If you have, declare today an introvert smile day and go for some practice.

A PRACTICAL IDEA *for* EXTROVERTS

Wonder what an interesting extrovert/introvert fusion strategy might be for an extrovert. And let me know what you come up with!

WALKING SLOW

*E*arly this morning, I was at the gym, going around the running track really slowly. By really slowly, I mean slower than a stroll. It's a pace that probably looks like Buddhist meditation walking. Nobody seemed to notice. It's slow enough that one time somebody did ask me if I was okay as he passed me. Not sure what he was thinking. Maybe I looked like my battery was dying. Years ago, I studied tai chi. There was a period when I'd go out into my neighborhood doing an even slower walk. I quit that, because I was afraid somebody really would turn me in for looking too strange.

Recently I got a note from an *Introvert Energizer* reader describing her slower pace (than her extrovert husband's). She said she finds it hard to get going in the morning. One thing she does about it is to sleep until she wakes up with no alarm and to have breakfast before she showers. I share her experience with getting going in the morning. One thing that helps me is to start the day by doing nothing. Often I lie in bed for a few minutes after I wake up, clueless on purpose about what I'm going to do next. When I get up, I follow my body around for a few minutes, letting it putter. Before long, I seem to get my bearing, without trying much. Starting the day not in a hurry feels comfortable, even when I have to be somewhere at a specific time.

Introvert bodies are designed for a slower pace. Maybe it's because, as brain researchers explain, our longer brain pathways require more processing time than extroverts'. But the reward is that it integrates complex intellectual and emotional information more easily. It's actually harder for introverts to move our bodies, because we predominate on the side of the autonomic nervous system (the parasympathetic) that requires conscious thought. We have to decide to move. Evidently extroverts "just do it." :-) And the key neurotransmitter in our brains, which is acetylcholine, works along the same lines. It says, "Let's think about it," no need to rush into something, versus the extrovert neurotransmitter, dopamine, which goes, essentially, "If it feels good, do it!"

I started my Buddhist walking workouts a few years ago as an introvert experiment. I think I was tired of decades of gearing myself up for aerobic exercise and curious about how slow I'd go if I wasn't pushing myself. It turned out to be pretty slow! The experiment has turned into a habit. I feel a little guilty about my lack of aerobic exercise. (I notice the exercise experts aren't in agreement about it these days, though, so who knows what to think?) I don't really know what it's doing for my body to meander around the track. But I love going to the gym to slow down.

End of food for thought, on to a practical idea:

A Practical Idea *for* Introverts *and* Extroverts

Take yourself on a slow walk. See what you notice.

THAT INNER (INTROVERT) CHILD

*L*ately I've had several conversations with people about their introverted kids. I always recommend Marti Olsen Laney's book *The Hidden Gifts of the Introverted Child—Helping Your Child Thrive in an Extroverted World*. And I always add that I think the book is great for adult introverts, too, as a way to get perspective on who you were as an introvert kid. I've been talking about it enough that I got reinterested in my own life as an introvert kid and decided to give *The Hidden Gifts* another look.

I went straight to Laney's list of the gifts:

- Introverts have rich inner lives.

- Innies know how to smell the roses.

- Innies have a love of learning.

- Introverts think outside the box.

- Introverts excel in the creative arts.

- Introverts have a high emotional IQ.

- Introverts are gifted in the art of conversation.

- Introverts enjoy their own company.

- Introverts develop healthy habits.

- Introverts are good citizens.

I was looking to see how much of this description I could relate to in remembering myself as a child. I find the language somewhat fanciful. At first, I identified with maybe half the characteristics. I decided to reread the explanations of each one and, to my surprise, found a way to identify with the whole list. The last time I did this, I don't think it was 100 percent. Maybe I was in the mood to be convinced this time around, but I liked the feeling.

The first chapters of this book focus on the physiology of introverts and extroverts. It includes discussion on how the brain and nervous system—and the whole body—behave in little introverts and extroverts. This time as I read about the gifts of introverted children, I was struck with how concretely they can be connected to the physical traits. Introvert kids know how to "smell the roses," because their busy brains, always processing what they're experiencing, don't need much outside stimulation to stay occupied.

Introvert kids tend to have high emotional IQs, because their inner focus gives them access to their feelings, which they process and integrate, and which tends to create empathy for others. Introverts are dominant on the side of the nervous system that says slow down, relax, and take it easy, so introvert kids tend to be easier on their bodies. And introvert brains are designed to think before acting, so little introverts have a natural potential to develop healthy habits.

As for myself, this latest review of myself as a young introvert has resolved my softball guilt. I always dreaded those summer softball games that would get going in somebody's yard. In fact, I hated them to the point that I wouldn't play. I'd pick being seen as a party pooper over playing. I much preferred practicing backbends and other gymnastic feats with my friend Joycie in my own backyard. It's a vague way I've thought there was something wrong with me. Why didn't I like softball?!

Now I'm thinking it's just fine that I didn't. Thousands of little introverts may play softball with gusto. But I can also make the case for a team sport that requires your body to think on its feet not being a little introvert's idea of a good time. And I'm going with it.

End of food for thought, on to a practical idea:

A PRACTICAL IDEA *for* INTROVERTS

Think about reading *The Hidden Gifts of the Introvert Child* as a way to reflect on your childhood. Or muse about yourself and Laney's list of introvert gifts.

A Practical Idea *for* Extroverts

Think of a young introvert in your life and find a way to send her
or him a vote of confidence.

Introvert
on the Road

A couple weeks ago I took a short solo road trip to visit my sister and my brother, a little fewer than four hundred miles one way. I was leaving on Friday morning, and, as life would have it, Thursday was a very busy day into the evening. My plan was to get on the road by about 9:00 a.m. I was pretty determined and pretty happy about the plan. But before I went to bed Thursday night, I had that familiar feeling of my plan and reality not quite matching up. To be out the door by 9:00 the next morning would be a small miracle and probably not very fun.

I remember reading an article a few years ago about the busyness of life in the United States. It told about how the comedian Ellen DeGeneres coined the term "Too Busy Syndrome" (TBS) and reported that before the 2004 presidential election, a poll of swing voters had rated not having enough free time as their biggest concern, ahead of the economy, health care, or the war in Iraq. Thursday night, I diagnosed myself with TBS, for sure. I woke up the next morning at 6:00, half determined and half pretending that I'd leave by 9:00.

After a couple hours of pretending and determination, I noticed I wasn't having much fun and had a moment of truth. It was that I could start having fun if I slowed down and if I remembered that I was on a mini-vacation and that *I* was the one who'd decided to leave by 9:00. So I slowed down and started having fun.

I let myself pack more stuff than I would probably use, including a cheerfully embarrassing number of books, to allow for freedom of choice and spontaneity and unexpected bursts of creativity. (How thorough of me!) I let myself think about not just leaving. I thought about coming back, so I could be more ready for life after my mini-vacation. I called a friend who's recuperating from surgery. He'd been on my mind for days, but I'd been too busy suffering from TBS to call him. I even deboned a leftover chicken and put the meat in the freezer instead of throwing it away because I was in too much of a hurry.

I left at noon instead of 9:00. I was in such a state of "beauty and order" by the time the car was packed, it was almost hard to leave. And I was smiling.

Introvert bodies, as I'm fond of pointing out, are designed to operate most naturally at a slower pace than extroverts'. Our nervous systems like to take it easy. TBS is not an introvert body's preferred syndrome.

I got on the road and realized I was on a roll with taking it easy. When

I remembered I should call my sister to let her know I was three hours behind my original plan, I found myself pulling over instead of nervously breaking my intention to not use my cell phone while driving. I drove the speed limit the whole way without feeling guilty for going "too slow."

Four days later, on my way back, I reminded myself I was still on vacation and hung out for two and a half hours during my lunch stop, reading, daydreaming, planning. It was dark when I got into town, but I didn't mind.

End of food for thought, on to a practical idea:

A PRACTICAL IDEA *for* INTROVERTS *and* EXTROVERTS

Diagnose yourself—are you suffering from TBS? If you are, take two aspirin and go straight to bed. :-)

"What Shall I Do with All My Books?"

A couple days ago, I was looking for pictures of famous introverts for a Powerpoint presentation I'm creating. I found a beauty of Abraham Lincoln sitting in a chair, with a young boy standing next to him. They're both focused on a big book Lincoln is paging through on his lap. They seem engrossed. There's a quiet introvert air about the image.

It got me thinking about introverts and books. I, myself, am addicted to books. Years ago, I typed up an excerpt from something—I have no idea of the source—that starts out, "'What shall I do with all my books?' was the question. 'Read them,' sobered the questioner. 'But if you cannot read them, at any rate handle them, and, as it were, fondle them. . . .'" It gives permission to read a sentence here, a sentence there, to arrange your books how you like them, to keep track of them and "if they cannot be your friends, let them at any rate be your acquaintances. . . ." I hang onto this excerpt for reassurance.

I grew up in a house full of books, with two introverted parents. And one of my strongest memories of visiting my grandparents every summer is of the floor-to-ceiling wall of books in their living room. It seemed gigantic. I wasn't just surrounded by books, I read them. I grew to depend on them for stimulation and inspiration, living on the edge of town in our little house on the prairie, pastures and fields right out the back door. I think it was a good combination for my young introvert self—easy access to good reading and the big quietness of the prairie right out the door, a balance to the almost-constant extroversion of life in the middle of lots of sisters and brothers.

I guess introverts are blessed when it comes to books. The blood flow in our brains takes a path that spends a lot of time up in the front, a complex territory that loves information and making sense of it. Introvert brains can (truly) spend endless amounts of time imagining, generating ideas, playing with options, making plans, rehearsing scenarios, thinking and thinking and thinking. We get "hap hits" (chemical "hits" of happiness) from it, all without moving an inch. No wonder I'm addicted to books. They provide endless material for what my brain likes to do. Extrovert brains get their hap hits much more easily from having their senses stimulated, *doing* things, not just thinking about them.

But, of course, addiction has its dark side. When I was a kid, there were books, so I read them. These many years later, it's more complex.

146

Books are small; there's always room for one more. :-) It's said that extroverts tend to have more friends than introverts, that extroverts will consider someone a friend an introvert might call an acquaintance. For me, with books, it's the opposite. Be a book of the right subject (and there are many), and you can be my friend—even after five minutes.

So I live with hundreds of friends, and more are on the way, no doubt. But I don't take my friendships lightly. Sometimes it makes being in a crowd of strangers feel like a relief! I enjoy my books for their very presence, for the possibilities they hold to inform me, to comfort me, to surprise me, to stimulate me, to support me, to keep me connected to the big pulse of life. I go to that excerpt to reassure myself, first of all, that it's a fine thing to be so in love with books, but also to remind myself that my hundreds of friends are patient, not at all offended by the word "acquaintance," and always happy to be fondled.

End of food for thought, on to some practical ideas:

A PRACTICAL IDEA *for* INTROVERTS

Think about yourself and books: are they your friends? If they are, spend a little time fondling them and see what you notice.

A PRACTICAL IDEA *for* EXTROVERTS

Be curious about yourself and reading. I know extroverts
who are voracious readers. What do you like about it?
What don't you like about it?

THE INTROVERT WITH
THE KITCHEN TIMER

For some time now, I've been interested in a technique called *kaizen*. It's a Japanese word that means something like "small steps for continual improvement." Most people I mention it to, if they've heard of *kaizen* at all, know about it as something connected with the business world. And it's true. The strategy of performing many small steps rather than big radical innovations developed in U.S. manufacturing during World War II out of necessity. And it gets credit for a big increase in America's manufacturing capacity during that time (evidently considered not a small factor in the Allied victory).

After the war, it was introduced to Japan as American forces helped Japan start rebuilding. The Japanese business world was receptive, began using it very successfully, and eventually gave it the name *kaizen*. In the meantime, once the war was over, this strategy of making small changes was ignored in America. It wasn't until the 1980s that it began to come back into the U.S. business world.

But back to me and *kaizen*. Many years ago, an American psychologist named Robert Maurer starting applying *kaizen* on a personal level. A few years ago, he published a book called *One Small Step Can Change Your Life—The Kaizen Way*. I've been working with it.

I love how creative human beings are. Now, with so much new brain research, we've discovered that this *kaizen* technique—tiny steps in a direction you want to go—works so well because it keeps us out of the amygdala, the part of the brain that triggers fear. Here's a quote from Maurer: "Small, easily achievable goals—such as picking up and storing just one paper clip on a chronically messy desk—let you tiptoe right past the amygdala, keeping it asleep and unable to set off alarm bells. As your small steps continue and your cortex starts working, the brain begins to create 'software' for your desired change, actually laying down new neural pathways and building new habits."

Maurer's book, appropriately small, :-) teaches how to apply *kaizen* by using small questions, small thoughts, small actions, small problems, small rewards, and small moments to create not-small changes in your life.

The not-small issue I'm experimenting with is my tendency to dive deeply into things. I've written about it before. On the one hand, it's satisfying. I don't worry about getting bored, because virtually anything I'm interested in can be explored endlessly. At one time, I probably unconsciously considered it part of what was wrong with me: automatically tending to linger on things, to ask a lot of questions, to want to know more, to think about my experiences intently. Usually it seemed there wasn't enough time and my pace wasn't fast enough.

Now, I'm so much more a conscious introvert, I get that it's normal for me. On a continuum, extroverts tend toward the breadth end, while introverts like depth. Introvert brains love to concentrate, and we gravitate toward thorough. The extroverts in the group might like to see as many animals at the zoo as they can. Me, I'd rather park myself by the river otters—but there aren't any chairs. :-)

Even if it's normal, this is no small issue for me. The minute I focus on something, I start feeling that depth tendency. And maybe I have an unusually serious case of depth-itis. But we live in a world that's generally more into breadth than depth. So it still often feels like there isn't enough time and my pace isn't fast enough. It's a starting and stopping challenge. I can be afraid to start something, because when you jump off the deep end, there you are in the deep end: wanting to think about something for a few hours instead of a few minutes. Same with conversations, if they're about something I'm interested in. And if one article on cooking a turkey is good, three or four are better.

Then, once I've made the dive, how to stop? How to get back up to the surface? What if I forget to buy the turkey, because I'm still studying the pros and cons of brining it? *Kaizen* to the rescue! Or probably sort-of *kaizen*. I'm still too much of a rookie to be a good judge. And if moving one paper clip is *kaizen*, I may be expecting too much from my amygdala.

But here's how it goes. When I'm putting off starting something, I get out the kitchen timer and set it for ten or even twenty minutes. (This is not a brilliant new idea that came to me. For a long time, I've known about the strategy of deciding to do something for just a few minutes as a way to break through being paralyzed.) The deal I make with myself is to focus on the activity until the timer rings, without thinking about what happens next. When it rings, sometimes I just know I want to continue. I'm on a roll, and I reset the timer. If I don't know, I take a few solid breaths and ask myself a question, probably a bona fide (that is, small) *kaizen* question: do I want to keep going? If the answer is no, I do my best to respect it and stop.

Managing depth-itis will no doubt continue to be one of my jobs. And I'm hanging onto all my turkey information. But thanks to the little timer, I notice starting and stopping doesn't have to be quite such a big deal after all.

End of food for thought, on to a practical idea:

A PRACTICAL IDEA *for* INTROVERTS *and* EXTROVERTS

Check out *One Small Step Can Change Your Life—The Kaizen Way,* by Robert Maurer, PhD. If you already know about *kaizen,* design yourself a new little *kaizen* project.

Introvert Parents
off the Hook

t's been a couple years since I first heard about research that says we need at least eight hugs a day—and twelve is even better—to thrive. I'm definitely interested in thriving, but I'm not an automatic hugger, so I've been chewing on this new hugging mandate.

Until I was in my mid-twenties, I don't think I ever thought about myself and hugging. But as I started being in groups where it was a norm to hug, I did think about it—and had to figure out some strategies! I don't know that I've exactly blamed my parents for my lack-of-hugging tendency, but for all these years, they certainly come to mind when I think about it. Being the oldest kid of seven, I was in a good position to watch what was going on in our household. What I noticed was that my parents seemed naturally affectionate with my sisters and brothers, up to a certain age. Of course, once our family got to pack size, it wasn't as if everybody was getting held or touched all the time. But my memory is of the little kids getting plenty of it.

I'm not sure of the age, but probably by the time we were six or seven, things changed. "Big kids" didn't get much physical affection. So I grew, I suppose, to not expect it and even to be self-conscious if much hugging was going on around me. And, of course, I grew up on the prairie, in a culture that was mainly just fine with minimal display of affection—lots of Scandinavian and German salt-of-the-earth people.

But I've had a revelation. If my parents were introverts, it makes sense that we didn't get smothered with physical affection. Introverts have a strong sense of personal space. We need it to thrive. For one thing, our bodies spend energy just being around other people, even if we're not interacting with them.

For another, to process all that's continually going on in our busy brains, we need to block out external stimulation enough to turn our attention inward. And third, introvert bodies can't generate new energy unless the external environment is shut out. All of which is basically foreign to the extrovert experience. Extroverts, for instance, get energy from being around other people. Even standing or sitting too close to introverts—much less *hugging* them—sucks up our energy! (This physical difference between introverts and extroverts no doubt contributes to the stereotype of introverts being standoffish.)

And I don't make the assumption that all introverts belong in the classification of hesitant hugger. Human beings, after all, are complex and diverse, and so are their environments. One of my best friends calls herself an introvert who hugs. But let's not forget these introvert physical realities.

And let's hear it for my introvert parents! They probably intuitively knew it was a good thing to cuddle up their babies and also enjoyed it. They gave all their children, introverts and extroverts alike, an environment to practice pretty nonstop extroverting. (A small house full of kids will do that.) Plus they respectfully gave us our personal space at an early age.

About getting those eight hugs a day. For one thing, I'm wondering if hugging yourself counts. :-) And I'm also wondering—seriously—if the finding of multiple hugs a day as important to thriving was made with any awareness of the physiology of temperament. Maybe introverts can thrive on five.

End of food for thought, on to some practical ideas:

A Practical Idea *for* Introverts

Think about yourself and hugging: Do you like it? Do you get eight a day? Was your family big into hugging?

A Practical Idea *for* Extroverts

Don't skimp on those hugs. You're a natural at it! And if you come upon someone who seems standoffish, consider the possibility that you're dealing with an introvert who's respecting your personal space.

Inside My Head, Reflecting

A few weeks ago, I came across a small empty picture frame in a drawer. There I was, back in touch with my family-pictures project. And here I am, still thinking about it and doing nothing. This isn't a new subject. More than ten years ago, in the middle of putting a new roof on our house, the roofers made a bad call on timing and found themselves in a downpour, minus a roof or any other protection for the house. All our family pictures, carefully displayed on second-floor walls, came down in the aftermath. They're still down. Hanging them again is one of the things on my long-term to-do list. :-)

A lot can happen in a family in a decade—graduations, marriages, deaths, births. The family-pictures project isn't just a matter of rehanging. Almost always when I get into facing up to it, I think of my friend

Inside My Head, Reflecting

Zoe's house. Zoe is an extrovert, and her house is brimming with family pictures. They're everywhere, and very engaging. When I'm there, I usually have the thought that I'd like everybody to leave so I could really look at all those pictures.

At least once a year, I deal with myself and the family pictures. Sometimes I calculate what season would be best to do them in. Sometimes I just feel guilty. Or overwhelmed. Or exasperated that I have a to-do list that goes on for years. (I now have a file of magazine articles about family pictures.)

One of my favorite quotes on introversion comes from *Gifts Differing,* a classic book about the Myers-Briggs Type Indicator, which tests for introvert/extrovert temperament. The quote is, "Introverts do their best work inside their heads, in reflection." I think it's an accurate statement. And I think if we took it to heart, we'd be coming up with ways to collect what goes on inside introvert heads better.

But about my project. Here's what I know. Even though I take comfort in this generalization about introverts—that our best work may not necessarily show up out in the world—it doesn't let me off the hook. And, of course, I know it's not for lack of caring that I haven't done it. The opposite is more true: I know my family to be so beautiful and so complex, maybe it's only the pictures I hold inside my head that can do this project justice.

But my grandbaby just turned two. Kindergarten pictures? No problemo—I'm getting ready. :-)

End of food for thought, on to some practical ideas:

SOME PRACTICAL IDEAS *for* INTROVERTS

Take a day to appreciate, all day, that you're blessed
with a head that's good at reflecting.

If you have one, take your long-term to-do list out
for lunch and make it smaller.

SOME PRACTICAL IDEAS *for* EXTROVERTS

Carve out some time to be inside your head reflecting,
for no particular reason.

If you have one, take your long-term to-do list out
for lunch and make it smaller.

INTROVERT ON STAYCATION

O ver Labor Day weekend, I went on staycation. (From Wikipedia, I found out "staycation" officially qualifies as a "neologism," a new word or phrase. Staycation means being on vacation, essentially, while staying home.) My brother came to town to vacation with a couple friends, and he invited me to join the fun. For four days, I slept at home, but during the day I tromped around among hundreds or thousands of people. This was an extroverting staycation. And I'm still here to tell the story. :-)

The warm-up was Thursday night: supper at a big, noisy pizza place, with family. It was so crowded we had to park in a shopping mall down the road from the restaurant. Friday was the Minnesota State Fair, an annual twelve-day event covering 320 acres and averaging 150,000 visitors a day. Saturday was the Minnesota Science Museum, to see the visiting exhibit of the Dead Sea Scrolls. The Science Museum is one of the few in the world that's been allowed to display the two-thousand-year-old fragments, so it's popular. To regulate traffic, curators let 150 people start viewing the exhibit every fifteen minutes. The fragments are tiny, but the exhibit isn't. It takes a couple hours to do it justice.

Sunday was the Minnesota Zoo, more hundreds of acres and some seven thousand people, a crowd full of lively kids. Monday, last but not least, was major league baseball: a Minnesota Twins game, 40,258 fans in the new outdoor stadium, including riding in on the jam-packed, standing-room-only light rail.

I emerged from all this fun remarkably intact. To be sure, it wasn't quite business as usual for at least a couple days afterward, but I expected worse. How did I pull it off, I wonder? (Even extroverts around me were sounding a little squeamish at the thought of that much stimulation in one weekend.)

The short answer might be mind over matter. I'd been looking forward to this little vacation with my brother all summer. I really wanted to do it. But I think I was being a strategic introvert, too. For one thing, besides the pizza supper, I'd decided everything was optional. I'd take it one day at a time. And the week before, I found myself cutting my activities down to a bare minimum.

Introverts like depth, and we like interacting one to one. I'd signed myself up for mingling with some two hundred thousand people! I think I intuitively decided to go with breadth. Every day, I noticed I'd announce I didn't really care what happened. Just doing it was my main goal. As soon as we got into the noisy pizza place Thursday night, I knew I wouldn't be trying to have much conversation with anybody. I watched, listened, ate pizza, and enjoyed being in the company of people I love.

At the State Fair, which has a reputation for sensory overstimulation by anybody's standards, I picked a partner in our group of six and stayed glued to her. I got to pet a newborn piglet for more than a moment, had a leisurely conversation with the woman in front of me as we waited in line twenty minutes to get coffee, and floated cheerfully along in the sea of humanity.

At the Dead Sea Scrolls, I concentrated. Even though I was surrounded by people, everybody doing their own improvised routes, I focused on the displays and came out essentially unjostled. Sunday at the zoo was a breeze. We were a group of four, nobody in a hurry, 143,000 fewer folks than at the fair, lots of fresh air and sunshine. And I kept my expectations low.

By the end of the third day, I was appreciating the notion of staycation. All this extroverting was getting balanced with coming home to rest. My introverted nervous system was having familiar downtime. I did the Twins game like a veteran. :-) I'm not a baseball fan, and it had been more than twenty years since I watched a game. But by this time, I'd gotten the hang of managing myself in a crowd. So I decided to smile, go with the flow, and really enjoy my bratwurst.

End of food for thought, on to a practical idea:

A PRACTICAL IDEA *for* INTROVERTS *and* EXTROVERTS

Think about a staycation. What would you do?

PEOPLE LOVERS

Here are synonyms for "extrovert" and "introvert" from the thesaurus section of Dictionary.com:

- Extrovert: outgoing, approachable, friendly, genial, kind, open, warm, sympathetic, gregarious, sociable, informal, expansive

- Introvert: loner, afraid, fearful, hesitant, modest, nervous, suspicious, unassertive, unsocial, unresponsive, recluse, narcissist

The day I looked, directly above them was an ad (that didn't look like an ad) that read: "Introvert = loser. Being yourself is not the Solution. It's the Problem. Learn to Change." A Web address followed.

Of course, I'm no stranger to the fact that "extrovert" has a more positive connotation than "introvert." But I wasn't expecting quite this much misconception from Dictionary.com in 2010. It's been close to a century since the psychoanalyst Carl Jung coined the two terms as healthy aspects of temperament. And it's almost that long since he and Sigmund Freud, another pioneering psychoanalyst, had theoretical differences and parted company, and Freud started using the concept of introversion as a negative, a misconception that obviously continues.

What surprised me even more, though, was something that came out of my mouth a couple days ago. Frances the Corgi (dog) had just met a new person. She was being her usual friendly, engaging self, so pleasantly distracting, in fact, that her new friend Kevin commented on it. Then, here's what I said: "She an extrovert—she loves people." Technically I was being accurate in how I know Frances. If a Myers-Briggs Type Indicator existed for dogs, I'm sure she'd come out an extrovert. And she does love people.

But as soon as I said, "She loves people," I felt betrayed by myself. It was over in a second. Frances went on to something else, and Kevin was able to concentrate. But I felt the disconnect between what I said and what I know to be true, which is that loving people has nothing to do with whether you're an introvert or an extrovert. *And* big differences may exist between how extroverts and introverts express love.

To get technical for a moment, neuroscience research is showing that the blood pathway of an extrovert's brain has much less internal stimuli than an introvert's, which means extroverts are constantly scanning the outside world for stimuli to interact with—and to prevent boredom. :-)

Introvert brains, on the other hand, are very busy with internal stimuli: more blood flow, higher activity in the frontal lobes, a longer pathway for the neurotransmitters to travel. And the pathway gets to the emotional center, the amygdala, last. So introverts tend to have delayed emotional responses. Introverts are looking to minimize external stimuli to prevent being overwhelmed. And this has nothing to do with shyness, which results from lack of confidence. I recently saw a statistic suggesting there are more shy extroverts than introverts.

If Frances were an introvert, instead of smiling broadly, wagging her tail like mad, barking, and exposing her belly for rubbing, she may have given Kevin a gentle wag and one lick and then followed him around, quietly watching. Meanwhile, remind me not to spend too much time poring over the thesaurus.

End of food for thought, on to a practical idea:

A Practical Idea *for* Introverts *and* Extroverts

Come up with five words that represent aspects of a healthy introverted temperament.

On Twitter

I got a note from an *Introvert Energizer* reader who's been thinking about introverts and Twitter: "I don't know, because I haven't done even an anecdotal study on this. All I know is that most people seem to like Twitter a lot, whereas a small minority of people find it completely off-putting. As an introvert, I am in the latter category, because I find it both boring and overstimulating at the same time. So it occurred to me that Twitter is probably great for people (extroverts) who seek and need lots of external stimulation, whereas introverted people who are already stimulated internally don't need that. Also, introverts like to go more in-depth on themes and ideas, and Twitter doesn't really accommodate that. On the other hand, maybe there are lots of introverts who like it for their own reasons. Who knows? Just something to think about."

Yes, something to think about, I thought, Twitter being only one tip of a big iceberg. It bothered me that I couldn't think about Twitter very well, because I know so little about it, including, of course, that I don't use it. I considered staying at my current level of denial and ignorance, but curiosity won out and I've spent a few hours reading about social media. Basic definition, encyclopedia-like information, mostly from Wikipedia. Besides "social media" itself, I looked up Twitter and things like "blog," "podcast," "wiki," "YouTube," and various other subcategories. It felt like getting to know a big extended family.

I was wowed by some of the statistics: Twitter, launched in 2006, evidently has some 190 million users from all over the world, generating 65 million "tweets" every day. As of 2007, a blog search engine was tracking more than 112 million blogs. And in May 2010, 14 billion videos were viewed through YouTube, which gets thirty-five *hours* of new videos uploaded to its site every minute. Yikes!

I remember switching from my beloved IBM Selectric typewriter to word processing. It was definitely a process, but I didn't look back. And I remember getting used to e-mail, a bigger paradigm shift for me. (And has it really been eighteen years?!) I started a LinkedIn profile a couple years ago, I think, but I haven't looked at it since I got distracted early on. I've had a copy of *Facebook For Dummies* for at least a year. I joined a website for Corgi dog lovers for about two weeks but backed out because of information/interaction overload.

I have a few people in my life (not sure if they're all introverts) who are still fairly or completely disinterested in using even e-mail. And I'm older than some of them. :-) Which may be just as well, because I hear it's becoming passé.

Here's what I know: Introverts do get depleted by too much external stimulation. We get overwhelmed by too much social engagement. (I had to quit that Corgi site because I found myself getting emotionally involved with practically every message I read, and there are a lot of Corgi lovers!) I remember hearing a leadership expert say he considers a lot of this technology "disconnected connection," which may be true.

I know I haven't given up on myself and social media. I can see *Facebook For Dummies* from where I'm sitting. And I know right where my LinkedIn file is. But I'm clear I won't be uploading anything to YouTube in the next few days.

End of food for thought, on to a practical idea:

A PRACTICAL IDEA *for* INTROVERTS *and* EXTROVERTS

Have a conversation with somebody about Twitter.

FRIENDSHIP BY PHONE

*T*his is about the challenge of pursuing friendship by phone. Paradoxically, even though I spend considerable satisfying time on the phone coaching, it isn't my first choice for staying connected with my family and friends.

Sunday morning, it was time to call my (introvert) friend Pat, after a couple months' break from our habit of every two weeks. I did it, but I almost put it off for another two weeks. I came home from the gym with thirty minutes before my window of opportunity. Pat lives in India, ten and a half time zones away, and there's a small period of time that works for both of us.

I once read a book about making small talk that called nonsmall talk "big talk." Introverts are known for not preferring small talk. The older I get, the less clear I am about what constitutes small talk, but in general, I'm not a big fan of it. (Where I grew up it was often called "shootin' the breeze.")

It isn't that I'd mind shootin' the breeze with Pat. After all, it had been weeks since we'd talked. Perfect would be hanging out with her in person for three or six hours, talking about life, big and small, but with probably more big talk than small. This morning it would have to be some of both, and we didn't have hours. I felt tongue-tied. What to do? Should I sacrifice breakfast to get centered for this challenge?!

It's a common introvert tip to prepare for social encounters by making a list of things to talk about ahead of time. I've resisted that strategy, because it feels contrived and boring. But I think I'm softening up a little, because I've done it a few times lately, and it's not all that bad. I was feeling either/or: eat breakfast or strategize about my phone call. But I grabbed a piece of paper and brainstormed some small-talk topics. Lo and behold! I had time to make the list and to eat breakfast, too.

We talked for forty minutes. It wasn't perfect—too short, not in person—but it was wonderful in its own way. A blending of big and small talk. And I checked off every item on the small-talk to-do list. :-)

I think I have to trust that small talk and big talk can happen at the same time. I watch extroverts and introverts around me having short, seemingly meaningful conversations—and sometimes it's totally "small talk." (And yes, I know Skype may be a happy medium, but I'm not there yet.)

End of food for thought, on to a practical idea:

A Practical Idea *for* Introverts *and* Extroverts

Think about you and friendship by phone: Is it satisfying?
What could make it better?

FINAL THOUGHTS

he gifts of introversion are many! Introverts are likely to be responsible, flexible, independent, studious, and smart. We have a strong ability to concentrate. We're good observers, we feel experiences deeply, and we comprehend the vastness of any subject. We maintain long-term friendships and work well with others, especially one to one. We're creative and willing to make unpopular decisions, and, because of our keen powers of observation, we understand the complexity of the world and people. We're likely to be very self-aware and to have the capacity to bring a slower pace to life.

I hope you identify with this description, and I hope you love yourself in it. Envision a world where this combination of traits is held in high esteem. Envision yourself flourishing in this environment. The world is longing for more introvert energy. Cherish yours and share it with (introvert) gusto!

ABOUT THE AUTHOR

NANCY OKERLUND has successfully coached introverts for more than thirteen years and is the founder of the coaching company Introvert Energy. A conscious introvert with a master's degree in human development, she's certified by the Coaches Training Institute (CTI) and the International Coach Federation (ICF). She makes her home in Minneapolis, Minnesota.

PHOTOGRAPH BY ANN SILVER

Made in the USA
Charleston, SC
28 October 2011